The Long Walk Home

The Long Walk Home

Discovering the Fullness of Life in the Love of the Father

Matt Carter

B&H
PUBLISHING
NASHVILLE, TENNESSEE

978-1-4336-9064-8

Published by B&H Publishing Group
Nashville, Tennessee

Dewey Decimal Classification: 226.8
Subject Heading: PRODIGAL SON (PARABLE) / GOD-
ATTRIBUTES / LOVE

Cover design and illustration by Matt Lehman.
Photo © Blue Collectors / Stocksy

1 2 3 4 5 6 7 · 23 22 21 20 19

For my daughter Annie
I never could have fathomed the gift God gave me
when He gave me you, my only daughter. I simply
cannot imagine my life without you in it. You
are one of those rare souls that has the perfect
combination of beauty and strength. You're a lover
and a fighter for what is good and true and right.
I love you with all my heart, and I pray that God
uses your life to bring many prodigals home.

Contents

Introduction

Being a Christian is hard. There, I said it.

Some of you just read that first line and already are judging me.

Wait a minute, Matt; Jesus said, "My yoke is easy and my burden is light" (Matt. 11:30). And you know what? That's true. When I'm fully submitted to Jesus and walking well with Him, that verse makes all the sense in the world. My problem is that I have a pretty good track record of not consistently walking well with Jesus. That's when it gets hard. Not because of Him but because of me. Maybe that's not your story, but it's mine. Christianity is hard. Worth it, but hard.

There's an old Willie Nelson song that I remember hearing in my dad's pickup truck when I was a kid. Maybe you remember it. It's called "My Heroes Have Always Been Cowboys."

Why, for old Willie, have his heroes always been cowboys? According to those lyrics, it's probably not because of the horse or the hat or the gun but because cowboys live a life that makes sense to him. Willie lets us know that cowboys live a life of cold, lonely, nightmarish misery—and he can relate.

As a pastor for more than twenty years, I've been preaching the Bible for a long time—been reading it for even longer. And when it comes to my biblical heroes, the ones I have found over the years that I love the most, I love not because of the good they've done but, honestly, because of how they've failed. Why? Because I can relate.

I've personally never called down fire from heaven and burned up the offerings of pagan worshippers like Elijah. I've never parted the Red Sea or stood beside a burning bush like Moses. I've never walked down into the valley of the shadow of death and killed a nine-foot-tall giant like David. But, like Peter, I *have* tried to walk on water (yes, I tried it once) and instead sank like a rock. Just like Peter, with my actions, I have denied Christ—more than three times. Like Peter, I've run from my calling and just gone fishing when I should have been standing firm and faithful. I've always liked Peter, not because he wrote part of the Bible or because he was a stalwart of the early church, but because I can relate to this flawed, battered, and bruised man who desperately loved his Savior.

There's another guy in the Bible—I definitely wouldn't call him my hero, or really a hero at all, but I can certainly relate to him. You may have heard of this guy in some Sunday sermon or in a Sunday school flannel board lesson of your youth. People often refer to him as "the prodigal son."

If you grew up in church, you know the story, but if you didn't, here are the basic plot points. A young man, the young man we come to know later as the "prodigal," asks his dad for his inheritance, even though the old man is still alive. His father grants his wish, and the young man takes off to a foreign land where he squanders his inheritance and is forced to come home with his hat in his hand. That's actually *not* how the story ends, but I don't want to get too far ahead of myself.

When I was younger, I couldn't relate to this guy. I thought, *How stupid do you have to be to ask for, then take your entire inheritance and blow it being monumentally stupid? Who would do that to their father? What kind of idiot would make all those poor decisions?*

But now, years later, unfortunately I can relate to the prodigal more than I ever thought possible in my youth.

The older I get, the more I'm aware of my flaws, my sins, my failures, and my shortcomings. They're many and they're ugly. Am I an abject failure as a believer? No. Are the words of the Scripture that say He who began a good work in me will be faithful to complete it (see Phil. 1:6) true? For me, yes they are. Do I see the fruit of the Spirit in me, and by the grace of God is it increasing? Yep. BUT I also know that as a man with a few years and few failures under his belt, I read the Bible differently now. I read it not as a young, self-righteous punk who thought he had the world figured out, but rather as a flawed, sometimes weary soul desperately searching God's Word for every drop of grace that can be squeezed out of it.

If you're a Christian who has it all figured out, this book is not for you. If you're a Christian who has never really failed or fallen or struggled, there might be a better use for your time than reading these pages. But if like me, you love the Lord, but at times throughout your life you find yourself weary and broken, confused and questioning—maybe even hanging on by a thread—then this book *is* for you.

No matter how weary you are or how far you've fallen, your Father's love for you is greater than your wildest imagination. I wrote this book partly as therapy for myself and partly as a guide for people like us.

And hopefully it will guide you back into the arms of a loving Dad—maybe not the dad you had but the one you always longed for—a Dad who is ready to welcome you home, wipe you clean, and call you His beloved son or daughter.

CHAPTER 1

The Problem

One of my earliest memories was that of food and a great woman. It was 4:00 a.m. on Thanksgiving morning in 1978, and I was five years old. Dreary eyed and yawning, I got out of bed to go to the kitchen and get a glass of water. As I fumbled through the dark, I was surprised to hear noise coming from the kitchen that early in the morning. I walked farther down the hallway, shuffling my footie pajamas across the old hardwood floor, hoping I had simply imagined the sound.

Bang!

There it was again. My heart beat faster, and I was consumed by that sense of dread and helplessness only a five-year-old can feel in the dark. But then the smell hit me. Corn bread. Yes—it was the sweet smell of corn bread, mixed together with the aroma of onion and sage. Your mind is a powerful thing, and I've read somewhere that your sense of smell triggers the most powerful memories. To this day, every Thanksgiving when I smell corn bread, onions, and sage, I am transported back to that dark hallway, shuffling along in my footie pajamas.

My little stomach immediately came alive and began to rumble. I followed the smells and the sounds until I turned the corner from the hallway into the kitchen. As my eyes adjusted to the light, I saw her—my great-grandmother. I instantly realized what was making all that racket. She was only five feet tall, and she was standing on her toes, reaching into a cabinet to grab a bowl she couldn't quite reach, banging pots against one another in the process. The smells? She was preparing corn bread stuffing that would soon join the yet-uncooked turkey in the oven. I remember thinking something in that moment that has stuck with me ever since: *My great-grandmother is up at four in the morning to cook for me. She really must love me.* And oh, she did. My great-grandmother was crazy about me. She proved it time and time again, and I miss her.

Her name was Theodocia Blackburn, and she was born in 1902. She lived until the mid-90s, and I often think about the changes she saw in her lifetime. Cars, airplanes, television, air conditioning, spaceships, computers—it's staggering to think about how the world changed from her youth to her old age. Was hers the generation that saw the greatest change? Maybe, but there's another great woman I think might see an even greater change in her lifetime, and that's my daughter. If she lives to the age of her great-great-grandmother, what will she see? What changes in culture and technology will she experience? It's hard to imagine, but I would venture to guess it could be as dramatic, maybe even more so than any generation before hers.

My daughter was born in the year 2002. She will never know what it was like to live before computers, the Internet, social media, or smart phones. She has an access to the world with all of its allures that I simply could not have imagined as a teenager. She doesn't just hear her favorite pop stars on the radio, but through social media and the Internet, she has daily access to their words, their thoughts, their homes, and even the routine of their everyday lives in a way that was unthinkable just twenty years ago. The twenty-four-hour news cycle and social media platforms like Facebook and Twitter provide real-time access to current events that previous generations would have found unthinkable. Yes, most assuredly, as Bob Dylan wrote, "The times they are a-changin'."

Along with society, the American Christian move-ment is changing too. I pastor a church full of college kids and young adults, and I'm telling you, the church is changing. When I was growing up in somewhat rural East Texas, everyone went to church, or at least felt guilty when they didn't go. But today that simply isn't the case. I live in Austin, Texas, and the overwhelming majority of people I meet don't go to church, nor does the thought of attending one ever cross their mind. In my city, espe-cially in the urban core of Austin, most people you meet are skeptical—at best—when it comes to Christianity. At worst they're hostile toward the idea of the existence of a God, much less the One who asks us to surrender our whole life to Him.

One of the most challenging and truly interesting aspects of my job is pastoring millennials and helping them navigate this ever-changing cultural landscape. And one of the questions I'm trying to get to the bottom of is how this seismic cultural shift is affecting the current generation. While I'm no expert on millennials or generation Z, I pastor several thousand of them, and I'm the father of three teenagers. One of the greatest changes I see in young people today, compared to previous generations, is their innate skepticism of the basic tenets of Christian faith and, even more so, of the necessity of the church.

When I was growing up in the 80s, the theory of evolution was a subject addressed in just a paragraph or two in my science book. I remember vividly my teacher also putting forth the Genesis creation narrative as a completely acceptable option of belief. Today, every academic environment young people find themselves in takes evolution for granted as the origin of the universe, and the idea that God created everything in a matter of days is laughed off as an antiquated fairy tale.

Consider the current cultural debate on gender issues, same-sex attraction, and the biblical definition of marriage. Earlier generations of Christians were never questioned or challenged on what were then socially acceptable positions. Today, to be a follower of Christ who believes in the historical view of marriage means being thought of as outdated, unloving, or even bigoted.

What about the Christian view of Jesus being the only way a person can go to heaven? Several decades ago in America, the majority of society were identified as Bible-believing Christians, so to claim that Jesus is the only path to salvation cost you nothing. Yet in today's world of cultural tolerance, to believe or teach that Christ is the *only* path to God will draw instant and sometimes severe consequences.

Another aspect of change that makes a significantly more challenging environment for young people is that they are growing up in the age of social media. I laugh sometimes when I think about my adolescence. I was just a normal kid. I was average at everything—sports, academics, and physical appearance—and because I was just an average Joe, I wasn't very popular. I had friends, but I was definitely not a part of the "in" crowd. But as I look back on that time, what makes me laugh is that I was blissfully ignorant as to how popular or unpopular

I was. In today's society all a teenager or college student has to do is look at the number of followers they have on Instagram and they know exactly where they rank in regards to their social standing. We were the lucky ones.

In 1991, if a group of popular kids from my school were at a party and I wasn't invited, I had no idea. Today, the kid at home watching a movie with his parents knows exactly what the popular kids are doing because of their pics and videos being uploaded to Snapchat. Statistics show that this reality has created an environment where the younger generation is less happy and less content than possibly any generation before them.

Make no mistake, it's harder than it's been in a really long time to be a Christian, especially a young Christian—and many young people are facing challenges and being forced to answer questions about their faith that someone born in the twentieth century may not have ever had to deal with.

Questions like:

> *Since being a Christian in today's society creates such a cultural disadvantage, if I truly follow Christ, what will it cost me?*

In a world where Christian principles are rapidly becoming the exception and not the norm, am I willing to be thought of as weird or different or outdated?

And arguably the question the younger generation is asking more than any other:

If I go all-in with living out my Christian faith, am I missing out on the best that life has to offer?

These and other soul-searching questions are at the forefront of the hearts and minds of the Christians I encounter throughout my ministry, and in my opinion we are in a place of crisis in the church. It's been well documented that the younger generation of Christians is leaving the church in droves. There are a lot of theories for this reality, but I'm utterly convinced it's because more and more people—really people of all ages—are being forced to count the cost of living out their faith, and they are deciding that it's simply not worth it.

Four Reasons People Are Walking Away

1. Growing Up in a Christian Home Is Not Enough for Sustaining Faith

Just last year I learned through an internal study at The University of Texas at Austin that the number of college students identifying as Christian has dropped to an incredibly low percentage. And that decline isn't just in my city; it is pretty much the same across the country. While many factors contribute to this reality, one of the primary reasons leading to this rapid decline is that kids growing up in Christian homes are showing up to college, then walking away from the faith, and never turning back. Why? Because their faith never truly became their own.

In the Gospel of John, there's a moment where Jesus looks at a huge crowd of people who were following Him because He was feeding and healing them. He pauses, looks at the crowd, and exclaims, "Unless you eat My flesh and drink My blood, you can have no part of Me" (see John 6:53). The crowd didn't understand what He meant, and they were offended. So they all turned around and walked away. His disciples were standing there with their mouths wide open, stunned that the popularity of their leader just dropped by about 99 percent.

Jesus, unfazed, turned to his disciples and asked them a question: "Are you going to leave me too?" Peter answered, "Jesus, where are we going to go? You alone have the words of life." Why are so many people leaving the faith when they walk out the doors of their Christian homes? I think the answer is simple: they have not personally come to the conclusion that Peter did—that life is found in only one place, and that is Jesus. Just like the crowds, they haven't personally tasted and experienced the life-giving, world-changing love of Christ, so when mom and dad aren't there anymore, they walk away.

2. The Allure of the Things of the World

Another reason for the decline of Christianity in our society isn't just in the number of college freshman choosing not to live as a Christian but the increasing number of people of all generations who simply come to the conclusion that yes, following Christ means I am missing out on the best life has to offer. Of course, this is nothing new.

Jesus Himself told us that many so-called followers of Christ would get caught up in the "cares of the world and the deceitfulness of riches" (Matt. 13:22 ESV) and walk away, but in today's culture I'm seeing a disturbing trend. As each year passes, I see more and more people who once lived as Christ followers make the decision to leave the faith.

I could fill pages of this book telling you story after story of people in my church that started strong in their faith—they attended and served the church, strived for holiness, and worshipped the Lord with abandon, only to completely walk away from God a short time later. The reasons are countless, but there is always a similar theme. Their faith in Christ forced them to make choices they simply weren't willing to make, and they walked away.

I could tell you numerous stories of young women committed to singleness in Christ until they fell in love with a nonbeliever and left the faith because following Christ meant not getting married. I know dozens of young men who were committed to sexual purity until they grew weary of the fight, fell into temptation, and, instead of repenting, walked away from God altogether.

I have far too many examples of women who were sick and tired of staying in a marriage with a man who didn't meet the expectations they had for him when they walked down the aisle, so they decided to bail. When confronted by their believing friends about God's design for marriage, they make statements like "I know God wants me to be happy" so they chose divorce—then not only walk away from their marriage but also their faith.

I've even seen several businessmen throughout the years who spent their careers amassing power and wealth, and when they encountered the Scriptures about generosity, instead of changing their lives according to God's Word, they simply walked away to live the life they want, unhindered by the "chains" of Christianity.

At the heart of every one of those stories and the many others just like them is an ever-increasing theme in our society—people who once walked with God decided that the cost of obedience was too high, and a better, easier, more fulfilling life could be found outside the family of God.

3. The Shame of Failure

This is a big one, and it deeply saddens me. I can't tell you how many folks I've encountered who choose to walk away from their faith because of the shame of past or current sin. Most of these folks grew up in church, so they know what God expects of them. When God saves us from our sin, He calls us to lives of purity. So when sin enters into some folks' lives, especially a pattern of sin that keeps reoccurring, the weight of that guilt and shame causes them to just give up altogether and walk away.

I recently talked to a prominent leader of one of the largest mission-sending organizations in the world. I noticed over the last several years that the overwhelming majority of young people going into the mission field from our church are women. Young men who answer the call to foreign missions are growing increasingly rare. I asked him what is the number one reason young men aren't going into the mission field, and he answered without hesitation, "Pornography."

He told me that the question on their entrance form is no longer, "Have you looked at pornography?" but rather, "How often do you look at pornography?" So prevalent is this sin in our society that they no longer asked *if* it was occurring but *how often.* To me this is one of the saddest realities in Christianity. I am seeing more young people than I can recall, either because of the allure of sin or the overwhelming shame and guilt experienced because of their sin, simply quit fighting, give up, and walk away.

4. The Lack of True Examples of Committed Disciples

I remember being in seminary, and we were studying the book of 1 Timothy. My professor looked at us and made this statement, "The whole point of the book of 1 Timothy is that you can't have one foot in the kingdom and one foot in the world." In other words, the truest, most accurate definition of a Christian is a person who makes the decision that their life is not going to be built on Jesus + something else.

You see this in the life of the apostle Paul when he said, "I have counted all things as a loss compared to the surpassing value of knowing Christ Jesus my Lord" (see Phil. 3:8). Jesus, too, spoke of this reality when He said, "A man discovered a treasure in a field, and for the joy over discovering this treasure, sold everything in order to buy that field" (see Matt. 13:44). The point? When people truly encounter the life-giving, soul-changing love of Jesus, they turn their backs on the allures of the world and go all-in.

I'm personally convinced we live in a country where people who have counted all things as a loss for the sake of Christ are becoming a rare species. Our churches are full of folks who love Jesus, but He is just *a part* of their life. They make their families, their jobs, their hobbies, and their relationships the central pieces of their life and then come to church on Sunday and worship Jesus.

Why, then, are these all-in type of Christians becoming so rare? The answer is that people are coming to the conclusion there is a more fulfilling life for them outside of God's love. So instead of *first* pursing Christ, they pursue the stuff of the world, and the result is our culture has perilously few examples of people who model the soul-satisfying Christian life. When young Christians see the older generation prioritizing the world over Christ, what possible conclusion can they come to?

The Problem and the Solution

I'm no statistician. I'm just a pastor in the everyday trenches of the church, but in my opinion the allure of the world is the greatest challenge facing Christianity. People are asking these questions sooner and more often than possibly ever before: "If I follow Christ, what will it cost me? If I fully commit to Christ, am I missing out on life's best?" And they're coming to the wrong conclusion and choosing the world over Jesus.

The reason I wrote this book is to help Christians of all ages better answer those questions. What is the correct answer to that second question? The correct answer is a resounding no. There is not a better life waiting for you outside of the love of your Father. The Bible is screaming from the rooftops that the greatest and fullest experience of happiness and blessing is found in only one place, and that is in a both-feet, full-hearted, total-life commitment to the person of Jesus.

I also wrote this book because I've wrestled with all of the same questions you are asking. My story is a story of discovery—most often learning the hard way—that there is absolutely no better life for me outside the love of my heavenly Father. As a high school student I often watched the lives of my non-Christian friends and wondered deep down inside if by following Jesus, I was living a life that was not as fun or exciting as theirs. Sitting on the tailgate of my truck or on the locker room bench after football practice, I listened intently as my nonbelieving buddies told their stories of how far they had gone physically with a girl the night before, and I was curious. I was curious because I knew the Bible told me I was supposed to save myself for marriage. But man, their stories sounded like fun. I longed to experience what they experienced, and I wasn't sure I wanted to wait until I was twenty-four years old and married to find out.

During my college years I genuinely began to walk with Christ. As a freshman at Texas A&M University, Jesus won my heart, and I knew that I wanted to follow Him the rest of my life. Yet even in those days when I was caught up in my "first love" with Jesus, a small part of me saw the "fun" my nonbelieving buddies had at their parties, and it created in me a real sense of doubt. I secretly wondered if my commitments to purity and holiness were excluding me from some powerful and mind-blowing reality that Christians simply weren't allowed to experience.

Unfortunately, these questions lingered long after college was over. Secretly I questioned, "Is a lower standard of living because of my financial generosity to the church *really* worth it? Are integrity and holiness *really* the best avenues for the 'life abundant' that Jesus promised us?" I've had these and a thousand other questions just like them, and I have felt guilty. Guilty for those questions that kept popping up in my heart and guiltier after the times I decided to find out for myself the answers to these questions.

As I write this, I am aware that there is a good chance I have less life ahead of me than I do behind me. If I've learned anything, I've learned this: the idea that somehow we are missing out on life's best by staying in the confines of our Father's house and living by His design is a lie—and it's a lie that comes from the pit of hell. Where this lie comes from and why we fall for it are the subjects of the next chapter. For now let's finish this one by helping you discover if this book is truly for you.

Becoming the Sixth

There have been a handful of older men who have made a huge impact on my life and ministry. My pastor in college, Chris Osborne, taught me to love the Word of God and helped me discover its unique power in preaching. Bob Swan—the oldest living youth pastor and my first mentor in ministry—taught me that humility and service are the best ways to pastor people. And then there are John Piper and Louie Giglio. These two men have arguably made the greatest impact on my generation of believers than any others. John Piper is a pastor and theologian who has written some of the seminal books that have influenced many of the pastors who are leading the church today. He taught my generation that God wants our happiness and joy and that joy is best found in Him. Louie Giglio is the founder of the Passion Movement. Through him I learned the value of excellent, God-centered worship and its power to draw our hearts to God.

Most people from my generation encountered the ministry and preaching of John Piper from Louie's Passion Conferences. And I remember the first time I heard Dr. Piper. I was sitting in the seats at a Passion Conference, hearing this guy preach, and the next thing I know, I'm on the floor, on my knees, weeping from a gospel gut-punch that Piper had just delivered from the pulpit. I later asked a friend who knew both Louie and Dr. Piper how those two titans of the faith met, and it's a really cool story. It's so cool, in fact, that I wondered if it's the stuff of lore or urban legend, but the story has now come from some trusted sources. So before I go any further, let me give you some context.

Dr. Piper is the real deal. He's not Jesus, and he's not perfect. But he takes the Christian life as seriously as any human being I've ever met. He's sold millions of books, but he lives so modestly that you'd never know it. He gives the overwhelming majority of his money away, and his commitment to the words of Scripture is both challenging and convicting.

Louie Giglio had heard about this radical guy named John Piper and wanted to meet him. As the story goes, Louie walked into the cafeteria of the conference where they were both preaching and saw Dr. Piper sitting alone at a table eating his lunch. Louie approached him and said something to the effect of "Dr. Piper, I'm Louie Giglio, and I just want you to know that I don't know if there are more than five people in this country who live out the Christian faith the way you do."

Now, if somebody were to say that to me, I would be floored with honor. I would blush and say something to the effect of "Wow! Thank you. That means so much that you would say that about me." But that's not how Dr. Piper responded. When Louie made that statement, Dr. Piper paused, turned his gaze from his lunch, looked Louie in the eyes, and said, "Thank you, why don't you go and be the sixth?" What an amazing question. And it's *the* question at the heart of this book. Are you willing to be the sixth?

There's a song we've been singing lately at my church called "More like Jesus." Interestingly, it's from Passion Music, the guys from Louie's Passion City Church. One line in that bridge stands out to me: "This world is dying to know who You are." It stands out because unfortunately it's literally true.

I recently read a book titled *Them* by Senator Ben Sasse, a strong Christian from Nebraska. In his book he talks about the crisis of unhappiness currently facing our country. The book's thesis is that while we're living through a time of radical technological innovation that has made our lives easier than at any other time in our history, that same innovation isn't leading to greater connectedness or happiness. People are arguably more isolated and unhappy than ever before. He writes,

> We've become accustomed to instantaneous answers and moment to moment connectedness. The digital revolution is making possible what was unthinkable just fifty years ago. We're the richest, most comfortable, most connected people in human history, yet in the midst of this extraordinary prosperity we are also living through a crisis. Our communities are collapsing, and people are feeling more isolated, adrift and purposeless than ever before. Despite the astonishing medical advances and technological leaps of recent years, for the first time in our history, the average life span in America is

in *decline* for the third year in a row. The culprit: Suicide and alcohol/drug related overdoses. We're killing ourselves, both on purpose and accidentally. These aren't deaths from famine, poverty or war. We're literally dying of despair.[1]

"We're literally dying of despair." That line stopped me in my tracks. It's true. We're all looking for happiness, and the world is convinced that being a follower of a dude who lived two thousand years ago is the last place you can find it. But here's the question: How's that working out? What's the result of the world's pursuit of happiness apart from Jesus? Well, they aren't finding it. As a matter of fact, the world's pursuit of happiness is actually producing the opposite result: people are so full of despair that they're turning to alcohol and drugs at a record pace to numb the pain. On top of that, the number of suicides is skyrocketing. Yes, people are literally dying of despair. Why? Because they are looking for happiness in people, places, and things that simply can't produce it.

You see, two thousand years ago, the King of kings and the Lord of lords made a bold claim that the fullness of life can only be found in following Him, and following Him completely. Friends, we live in a culture of dying people who are desperate for a different way, but there's a problem—How is the world going to know or see that better way if there's not a generation of Christ followers willing to show them? How are we going to turn the tide of death and despair riddling our culture if Christians live no differently than the world?

I'm convinced that what this world needs is not going to be found in better preachers. Through podcasts we have hundreds of anointed preachers whom people have access to twenty-four hours a day, seven days a week. Yet people are dying of despair.

I don't think what the world needs is better church programs. The church has spent the past 120 years creating countless events, programs, and nonprofits in an effort to reach the world for Christ—and while those are all good things, the world is still dying of despair. I'm also convinced that the world doesn't need more megachurches. Megachurches with right priorities can be a great force for good in the world. But there are more megachurches today than at any other time in history, and at the same time there are, per capita, fewer people attending church than at any other time in our country's history. This world desperately needs to be shown a new way. More than new songs and preachers and programs, the world needs a new, fresh wave of ordinary people who make the decision to go all-in when it comes to following Christ. This world is desperate for a generation of believers who don't just make Jesus a part of their lives but passionately put Him first and show this world with their everyday lives that, yes, there is a better path—a path of peace and love and happiness.

That Passion Music song hit the nail on the head. This world is dying to know Jesus, and it needs people just like you to show them who He is. But before that will ever happen, you must first come to a place of absolute resolve on this question: *Am I missing out on life's best by following Christ?* My prayer is that the following chapters will help you answer that question once and for all, and as John Piper said, "Be the sixth." If you do, you'll become an agent of radical change our world so desperately needs.

The title of this book is *The Long Walk Home,* and I pray that regardless of where you are in your journey, the words in this book well help you come home and stay there. For many of us, it will be a hard journey, but it's a journey worth taking. I promise you.

CHAPTER 2

The Lie

I addressed in The first chapter that at the heart of the crisis in American Christianity is a question so many people must answer sooner and more often than generations before them. It's the question of whether we're missing out on life's best by following Christ. In the Gospel of Luke, Jesus shares a story about a young man who was wrestling with those same questions. It's the story of the prodigal son, and Jesus told this story to help us answer those questions correctly.

You see, one of the amazing things about Scripture is that although it was written two thousand years ago, its truths are timeless, and it's incredibly relevant. It accurately diagnoses modern-day questions. The Bible's ability to address the deepest problems of my heart is honestly one of the reasons I believe in God. How is a two-thousand-year-old Book so relevant? I recently heard a pastor say, "Every book I've ever read, I read it. But when it comes to the Bible, it reads me." That is why I'm convinced God wrote it, and He told this story because He knew His children would one day face a world where they would question whether following Him was our best choice in life.

The prodigal son is relevant for many of us because this young man's temptations are our temptations—his story, our story. And through it Jesus has two goals. First, He is painting a picture of how God deals with His sons and daughters who have entered into a season of rebellion. And second, I'm convinced, He tells this story as a cautionary tale. Far too many of us who love the Lord still walk the same road as the prodigal, and this story helps us see the folly of this young man's decisions. Throughout the rest of this book, we will look at this young man's journey verse by verse, part by part, in the hope that we can learn the lessons from the prodigal son's life without having to experience the gut-wrenching consequences for ourselves.

Before we move ahead, I know some of you have decided at this point that this book isn't for you. You decided that because we are going to accept the authority of the Bible, the lessons taught here might not work for you. But I want to reassure you that I have friends just like you in Austin. No, I don't know *you*, but I know many people like you who believe the Bible is on the same level with Aesop's Fables, *The Iliad,* or Shakespeare's plays—a book that's earned its place in history but a book like other books. And while I hope to persuade you that the Bible is not a normal book, that it contains literal words of life, I want to challenge you to listen to the words Jesus spoke thousands of years ago because you might be surprised at how much of your own story you can find in them.

How It All Began

If you aren't familiar with the story, or parable, of the prodigal son, it is a story about a young man who grew up on a farm alongside his father and older brother. Jesus begins the tale by getting right to the point: The younger brother isn't happy. He's discontent, and he's grown restless living the life he's always known. And he's about to make a radical decision. The young man decides to leave his father and brother and take off for a new city and a new life. It's a bold decision, but before he breaks the news to his family, he makes an even bolder, darker decision.

Watch what Jesus says in Luke 15:11–12:

> And He said, "A man had two sons. The younger of them said to his father, 'Father, give me the share of the estate that falls to me.' So he divided his wealth between them."

We learn in the first two sentences of the parable that not only did the young man inform his father that he was leaving home for a new life; but incredibly, before he left, he asked his dad if he could have his share of the inheritance. Like I said, that's bold.

Think about how painful that must have been for his father! It would have been hurtful enough for the young man to tell his dad he's leaving, but he doesn't stop there. He tells his dad he wants an early payout of his inheritance.

I think Jesus puts this detail in the story to show us the significance of the betrayal of this young man toward his father. Leaving the family to go to the faraway land is bad, but asking for an early inheritance? That's downright cruel. You see, history is full of people who stood to inherit fortunes from their parents and deep down, in places they don't like to talk about, secretly wished their parents would make an early exit from this life. That scenario is probably more common than we think, but for the most part sanity prevails, and those dark fantasies go unheeded. But, unfortunately, for some wayward souls the lure of easy wealth proves too much to bear, and they act.

Only a few days ago I read a story in the news of a young man in my hometown who hired a hit man to kill his father because he stood to inherit two million dollars. And while these dark stories are too common, who throughout history has actually had the audacity to walk right up to their father—who is still very much alive—and say, "Hey Dad, not only am I going to leave you, but can you please give me my inheritance now?" By asking that question, he was basically saying, "Dad, I kind of wish you were dead. I'd rather have your money than you."

The hurt and the pain the father must have felt in that moment will be the discussion of another chapter, but this situation brings us to some all-important questions: What would bring a son to make such a shocking request of his father? What was the internal dialogue occurring in the heart and mind of this young man that led him to have such disregard for his relationship with his dad?

If you're anything like me, when you read the story of the prodigal son, you rush past this important question in order to move quickly to the end of the story. I get it; I've done it myself. Most pastors who preach on this parable rush to the grand finale where we see one of the greatest pictures of God's grace and love in all of the Bible. But in doing so, we miss one of the most crucial questions that helps us get to the heart of this story: *Why did the younger son choose to leave in the first place?*

While Jesus is not explicit in describing the younger brother's motivation, to me, there seems to be only one logical conclusion. Somewhere along the way in this young man's story, his eyes started looking toward the horizon and saw the bright lights of the city in the distance. And in the mundane, daily routine of his life on the farm, a question started creeping up from deep within his heart. It's the question I talked about in the first chapter and one that lurks in many of your hearts even now as you read this book: Is there a better life out there that I am completely missing out on by staying here in this place, being an obedient son or daughter of God?

For the prodigal, at some point the internal questioning resolves into an answer. The young man concludes that the answer must be *yes*—there *must* be a better life waiting for him outside his father's house, and he decides to act. He summons the courage, approaches his father, and asks for the cash. And incredibly the father agrees. So with a suitcase full of money, he takes off on his own to a new city, unhindered by the "chains" of the only life he had ever known.

We Are the Prodigal Son

When I was a kid, *before* I made my share of really bad decisions, when I would hear this story told from the pulpits and Sunday school classes of my small-town Baptist church, my typical reaction was not one of understanding but of judgment. I remember thinking to myself, *How dumb can this guy be?* As a "good kid" raised in a "good family," I thought harshly of this young man who discarded his father just to live an easy life of pleasure.

But now, as a grown man with plenty of trips to the faraway land under my belt, I'm not so quick to judge. Candidly, as I look back on what motivated *me* to turn my back on my heavenly Father and walk down the road toward sin, I now realize it was because I was asking the same questions as the prodigal. *Is there a better life for me outside of the love of my Father's house? If I really go all-in with this Christian life thing, am I missing out on life's best?* And when I became convinced that life's best was found in some other place, I took off.

One of the things that's important for us to get to the bottom of is why we start to ask those questions in the first place. Seriously, if life with God is *so* good and satisfying, why in the world are we tempted to leave Him for what we think are greener pastures? Part of the answer is our flesh. We're made of it, and for the most part our flesh is stupid, constantly longing for things that God says we shouldn't have. But the other answer is a little more hidden.

While it's true that you and I fall into sin because of our own fleshly desires, Jesus tells us that there's another source that causes us to question if life's best is found in obedience to God. His name is Satan.

For us to get to the bottom of how Satan works in our lives, I want to ask you a question. Have you ever been lied to? Most of us have and it hurts. The reason lies hurt so much is because at the end of the day we put our trust in the words of another person—then make decisions based on that word—only to find out that the thing we put our trust in was a big, fat lie.

I've been lied to many times in my life, but one particular lie stands out because of the hurt and embarrassment it caused me. Let me explain. The summer before my senior year in high school I worked at a Christian summer camp in East Texas. My job that summer was to run the rifle range where the camp counselors (mostly college students) would bring the campers and shoot .22 rifles. Looking back, it seems pretty ridiculous to put a seventeen-year-old kid in charge of a bunch of ten-year-olds on a shooting range, but hey, I grew up hunting, so I guess I was qualified.

On the first morning I cleaned the guns, placed the targets on the boards at the end of the range, and waited patiently for my first group of kids to arrive. As I sat there, I heard the telltale sound of kids screaming, and I looked up to see a college girl leading a group of campers down the path toward the shooting range. She was really pretty, and I remember thinking to myself, *This is going to be a great summer.*

I got the kids set up, and I remember doing my best to keep the kids from shooting one another, but I was distracted. I was trying to do my job, but I was also doing everything in my power to impress this college girl. I smiled a lot and made the kids laugh, hoping she would notice my obvious charm and small-town country wit. Well, I guess it worked, because at the end of our session, this girl walked up to me and asked for my name. I told her, and she asked me if I wanted to hang out later that night during her free time. I was beyond pumped! A college girl wanted to hang out with *me*?

To make a really long story short, we started dating; and at the end of the summer, we decided to continue the relationship. I was a senior in high school, and she was a sophomore at a college in deep East Texas, but we really liked each other and tried our best to make it work. We eventually broke up, and I want to tell you about a particular night that was the beginning of the end.

Halloween was approaching, and her sorority was having their annual Halloween party. A few weeks before the event, she called and asked if I could come with her. I agreed, but then she informed me that she wanted me to wear a particular costume. I answered, "Of course, anything you want," and that's when things started getting uncomfortable. I asked her what she wanted me to wear, and she said, "I've always wanted to dress up as Tinker Bell, and I think it would be great if you could wear a Peter Pan costume." As soon as those words came out of her mouth, my palms instantly began to sweat, and a thousand questions raced through my mind. *Doesn't*

Peter Pan wear tights? Green tights nonetheless? This girl wants me to show up at a college party wearing green tights?

I began to protest and begged her to let me dress up as Captain Hook, but she was having none of it. I was too young and insecure to tell a college girl no, so Peter Pan it was. Before I hung up the phone, I remember asking her one final question, "Hey, I'm a high school kid that's going to be in green tights. Are the other guys there going to be dressed up as well?" She assured me that every guy there would be in costume, *and* all of her girlfriends would be so impressed that I was secure enough in my manliness to show up dressed like Peter Pan.

So the weeks passed. I bought the costume, and on the day of the party I drove to her school. What occurred next can best be described as my worst nightmare. As the years have passed since that night, I've often been asked what was the most embarrassing moment of my life? Every time I tell this story. I can't tell you how many times over the years I've woken up in the middle of the night in a cold sweat thinking about the moment I walked into my first college sorority party wearing green tights and a feathered cap.

Why, you ask, is this the most embarrassing moment of my life? Well, when I walked through the door with Tinkerbell on my arm, I quickly discovered that I was the *only* guy in the room wearing a costume. I stopped in my tracks, looked at her in horror and said, "Uh, I'm the only guy here wearing a costume. I thought this was a stinking costume party?" She immediately tried to comfort me, assuring me that all her girlfriends thought I was cute and super courageous. I didn't care because it quickly became obvious to me that every single *college* guy at the party was staring at me and giggling at the high school kid that just walked in wearing tights. I looked her right in the eye, said, "I can't do this," turned around and walked out the door. Thankfully, our relationship never recovered.

I found out later that the Halloween party was "costume optional," and she absolutely knew that small, really important detail but chose not to tell me because she wanted to look cute for the party pics. And here's the all-important question: how did she talk a teenage high school kid into dressing up like Peter Pan? She lied.

Now, after lots of counseling and therapy, I can look back on that night and laugh. I'm pretty sure those party pics are lying around my house somewhere. If they ever show up on the Internet, well, you now know the story. But here's the reality of it all. I *never* would have made that decision if I had known the truth. I made a dumb decision that night for one reason. Somebody told me a lie and I believed it.

The Father of Lies

So that brings us back to Satan. The Scripture teaches us that besides our natural sinful desires, one of the primary reasons we choose to disobey God is Satan himself. So if we know that sin is wrong, how does Satan get us to choose that path? It's simple. He lies to us. And instead of believing God, we believe him, and then go out and make some monumentally stupid decisions.

Let's take a look at how Jesus described Satan. In John 8:44, Jesus speaks to a group of Pharisees and gives them some revealing insight into how Satan works:

You are of your father the devil, and you want to do the desires of your father. He was a murderer from the beginning, and does not stand in the truth because there is no truth in him. Whenever he speaks a lie, he speaks from his own nature, for *he is a liar and the father of lies.* (emphasis added)

What Jesus wanted you and me to know is that Satan by his nature is a liar. So if something is coming out of Satan's mouth, we can pretty much take to the bank that he's lying. And it's also important to understand that the number one way Satan deceives us is to get us *not* to believe what God says is right and good and best. And so when we fall to Satan's deceptions, just like me on Halloween of 1992, we make dumb decisions.

The thing you need to know about Satan is that his tactics haven't changed at all from the first moments of creation. God told Adam and Eve if they ate from the tree in the middle of the garden of Eden, they would die. Satan slithered up to them and told a bald-faced lie. He said, "If you eat from the fruit, you will not surely die."

They believed the lie, made a really dumb decision to eat the fruit, and death entered into the picture.

Satan is not stupid. He's actually quite the opposite; he's brilliant. And though he knows a day will come when he will be destroyed forever, until that day comes, he's going to inflict as much damage to you and me as he possibly can. What tactic will he use to bring his destruction into your life? The same tactics he used with Adam and Eve. He will lie to you.

I recently watched a movie (I had to turn it off because satanic stuff freaks me out) that did a really good job of displaying through cinema the predictable ploys of Satan. A young rock band was trying to make it big in the music industry. They had potential, but nothing was working out for them. Then one day after a terrible concert, Satan appeared to them and offered them the proverbial "deal with the devil." If they would worship him and do his bidding, he would give them untold success, fame, fortune, and influence. He promised them that everyone in the world would know their name. They took the deal and Satan delivered. They became the biggest rock band in the world. They lived in gorgeous houses and drove the best cars. They had their pick of any woman they wanted. They became wealthy beyond their wildest imagination, and for a while life was good. But on the front end Satan didn't tell them the consequences of their decision. Their decision to believe his lies led them to a place where their lives began to spiral and unravel toward a more destructive end than any of them could have foreseen.

I thought about it, and I realized this fictitious story was fairly accurate in depicting how Satan works. Though Jesus never mentions Satan as a character in the parable of the prodigal son, his influence is evident. And if you listen closely, you can hear the whisper of the father of lies in the young man's ear: "Hey, you're really missing out by living here with your dad. Don't you think life would be more fulfilling if you lived by your own rules and your own terms? Do you see that big city over there? That's where *real* life is happening. You should go! Get the money that belongs to you and go see for yourself!"

And in the first words of the story, Jesus tells us that the young man acted:

> The younger of them said to his father, "Father, give me the share of the estate

THE LONG WALK HOME

that falls to me." So he divided his wealth
between them. (Luke 15:12)

The prodigal son has been told a lie and becomes
convinced that a better life awaits him outside his father's
home, and he acts on the lie. In some ways it was an
innocent mistake. Just like all of us, he wanted happiness,
and he became convinced that happiness could be found
somewhere other than where he was. But what we will
see in the coming chapters, this one decision will bring
destruction to his soul that he could never have foreseen.

You see, this was such a successful tactic because
on the front end Satan never tells us about the consequences of trying to find happiness outside of God's
love. He always paints a rosy picture of sin. He makes it
look fun and pleasurable but conveniently leaves out the
fact that the Bible paints a much different picture.

Satan tells us that sin equals fun.

God's Word says sin equals death.

And when you think about it, every single time you
stand at the crossroads of sin and obedience, you are
ultimately making a decision: Am I going to believe what
God says is best or not? The result of that decision will

ultimately make the difference between finding real happiness or real misery.

The Power of Believing God

An interesting theme runs through the entire Bible. We find it in almost every book of Scripture from the Old to the New Testaments. It's the theme of believing God. In Genesis, God came to Abraham, really out of nowhere, and told him that he and his wife Sarah were going to have a baby in their old age. At first God's promise sounded ridiculous. Abraham said to God, "God, I'm an old man. I'm broken down and tired, and those days are long past me. And oh, by the way God, have you seen my wife? She's old and busted too." But then the Lord had him look at the night sky and said, "Abraham, see those stars? That's how many decedents you're going to have." What the Scripture says next is profound. The Bible tells us that "Abraham *believed God,* and it was credited to him as righteousness" (Rom. 4:3, emphasis added).

The New Testament tells a story of a Roman soldier whose servant was dying. He heard that Jesus was a man who healed the sick, so he approached Jesus and said, "Lord, my servant is sick. Can you heal him?" Jesus responded, "Take me to where he is and I will heal him." What the soldier said next, stopped Jesus in his tracks. The soldier responded, "You don't have to go to where he is. All You have to do is *say the word*, and *I know* he will be healed" (see Matt. 8:6–8). The Bible says that when the soldier said those words, Jesus "marveled." In other words, Jesus stood there in complete, jaw-dropping awe.

Jesus then turned to the crowds as if to say, "Hey, did you hear that? Did you hear what that guy just said? I have not seen *faith* like that in all of Israel." What in the world did this soldier do that caused Jesus to stand there in jaw-dropping awe? The soldier simply believed God. He believed that if Jesus *said the words*, it was absolutely going to happen. God loves it when His people believe Him. It's the simplest definition of a word that is used all the time in Scripture. It's called faith. When God says something, we believe it.

The Results of Believing God

As I look back on all the times in my life when just like the prodigal son I chose to walk down the path of sin, in each situation I was presented with a choice: the choice to believe the words of God or to believe the lies of Satan. And when you look at it like that, the choice seems so simple—so obvious. Of course I should believe God over Satan!

Then why so often do I not choose what God says is best? Because Satan is really good at what he does. He's the greatest deceiver in the history of the world and he's a master at presenting to us a picture of a better, fuller life apart from obedience to God, and far too often I stupidly took the bait. And every single time God's Word proved true. Sin never produced what it promised but only resulted in death, shame, and guilt.

On the other hand, sometimes, when presented with the allure of sin, I was able to see through the deception and believe God at His promises. Again, every time, God's Word was true. My obedience produced joy and life and peace.

And the sobering part of all of this: you will believe God one way or another. You will believe God before you sin and find life and joy and peace. Or you will choose sin and experience the consequences. Either way you will eventually believe Him. His words are true either way, and one of the beautiful aspects of this story is that we get to see the consequences of sin without having to experience them ourselves. The prodigal has bought the lie, and death is coming.

Friends, the reason Jesus told this parable (and why pastors like me continue to retell it) is to serve as a gentle and loving warning to all of us. Many of you, even now, are faced with the same dilemma as the prodigal. Maybe you haven't walked down the same road he did, but those same doubts he had are your doubts—those same questions are your questions. Is life's best found in a life of obedience to God? Am I missing out by truly following Christ?

If that is where you are, I want you to know something that maybe you wouldn't expect to hear from a pastor:

Those are legitimate questions—questions that you have to answer.

But they're also questions Satan desperately hopes you answer wrongly. My prayer for you is that the story of the prodigal son helps you see past those deceptive lies, believe God at His word, and stay at home where you belong.

Now I've been a pastor—and a sinner—long enough to know that many of you still aren't convinced. You hear me say that the best life has to offer is in obedience to God, but you just aren't sure if that's true. If that's you, I want you to know that I get it. I've been there. The world is pretty alluring, and on the surface it sure looks like a lot of fun. And here's the amazing thing: God isn't surprised by your doubts. He doesn't think less of you for having them. This powerful story can help you resolve those doubts without having to make the same mistakes the prodigal did.

Still others of you *have* bought the lie and have already taken the trip to the faraway land. If you're a child of God, my guess is that you are already discovering that Satan deceived you. My main aim for you in the following chapters is to show you that God is not done with you. There is still a story of beautiful hope and redemption waiting for you in the arms of a Father who has never given up on you or abandoned you.

And finally, a group of you reading this may have never wrestled with these questions and doubts about the goodness of God. You're following Him, and the prodigal son's questions and temptations aren't yours. If that's you, keep going! But know this: Satan probably knows your name, and if you are walking well with God, I can all but promise you he's eventually going to come after you. He hates nothing more than a child of God who walks in obedience to the One he hates. Read this story carefully. Heed its warnings. So when the attack eventually comes, and it will, you don't believe his lies. Regardless of where you are, let's follow the prodigal on his journey to the faraway land and see for ourselves how it all turns out.

CHAPTER 3

The Step

Every sin has a beginning—a first step. When you think about the times in your life where you've messed up and done something really stupid, one of the most important things to figure out is *why* you made that decision in the first place and what caused you to act. In the previous chapter we talked about how Satan loves to deceive us into thinking happiness is outside the love of the Father, but let's dig a little deeper into the deceptive nature of sin.

I grew up in a small, fairly rural town in East Texas, and so I spent a lot of my childhood in the woods. Some of my earliest memories are with my dad, fishing pole in my hand, standing by the numerous stock ponds at my granddad's farm. Now it's important to understand that when I say I went fishing, I'm not talking about your run-of-the-mill, everyday, put-a-worm-on-a-hook kind of fishing. I'm talking about the getting-really-serious, hard-core, redneck-skills kind of fishing. From an early age I could tell you the difference between a buzz and a crank bait, a Texas or Carolina worm rig, and the appropriate time of day to pull out the top water lures versus a rattle-trap. For the good country, churchgoing folk that we were, it wasn't a religion, but it was close.

And when you think about it, fishing, by its nature, is an act of deception. The whole point of fishing is to put something on the end of a line that *looks like* what a fish wants to eat. Let's take a buzz bait for example. It has a little head with a painted eye on it. Below the head it has a colorful little skirt that flows and sways in the water. And most importantly, it has this little bright and shiny, turning wheel that hangs off the top of the bait to churn the water as you reel it in.

So, when you throw that thing in the water, a fish sees it and thinks, *Sweet, that looks like lunch.* The fish swims for a while behind your lure trying to decide whether to take a bite. He may be leery at first, but then he sees the bait's little head and thinks, *Looks normal so far*. As he continues to follow the lure, he sees the colors, the flowing skirt, the churning of the water and decides deep down in his little fish soul, *I can't live without this any longer*, and he takes a bite.

But unfortunately for the fish, there's another part of every bait that is covered up by all the colors and skirts and shiny flashing objects. It's called a hook. The fish, that only a few seconds ago thought he was having a nice, midmorning snack, suddenly feels the pain of a sharp metal object piercing through his bottom lip. And the next thing he knows, he is being dragged out of the water, thrown in a cooler, filleted, covered with some cornmeal, fried in hot peanut oil, only to be eaten that night at a church fish fry.

Now, I don't know whether fish can think, but if they could, what do you think is going through their mind as they are being dragged by a razor-sharp hook toward places they never intended to go?

I would imagine it is something like, *Wow, I just made the greatest mistake of my life. What I thought was going to be a yummy snack has led me straight to my death.*

Friends, that is exactly what happens to believers when we sin. On the front end sin always looks enticing, fun, satisfying, and pleasurable. But just like that deceiving little fishing lure, there's always a hook, and sin will always take you to places you never intended to go.

King David's Great Sin

Let's take a minute and think about the story of King David and what has become known as his most notorious sin. For those of you who aren't familiar, the story I'm referring to is David's sin of adultery with Bathsheeba. The chapter title in my Bible is called "Bathsheeba, David's Great Sin." The Bible refers to his sin this way because in many ways this one decision David makes will ensure that his life will never be the same. For the man so famously referred to as "a man after God's own heart," this one trip to the faraway land of sin leads him down a path he never could have envisioned and would never fully recover from.

The story begins like this:

> Then it happened in the spring, at the time when kings go out to battle, that David sent Joab and his servants with him and all Israel, and they destroyed the sons of Ammon and besieged Rabbah. But David stayed at Jerusalem. Now when evening came David arose from his bed and walked around on the roof of the king's house, and from the roof he saw a woman bathing; and the woman was very beautiful in appearance. (2 Sam. 11:1–2)

The text sets the stage. It was springtime, a time when kings go out to battle (see 2 Sam. 11:1). That's an important part of the story. David was where he shouldn't have been! At this point in his life, David had fought and won battle after battle. As a shepherd boy he protected his sheep from lions and bears. As a young man, he walked down into the valley of death and defeated giants and great armies in the name of the Lord, but not on this night.

The Scripture said it was spring, the time when kings went out to battle, but not David. He was at home, alone, lying in bed. Maybe he was tired, maybe he was "burned out," maybe he was just bored with being king, but regardless, he wasn't where he was supposed to be.

It was a warm evening, and David got up to stretch his legs and look out over the city he had won for himself and his people with blood, sweat, and tears. When he peered over the edge of his palace, down below him was a woman bathing, and she was beautiful. The Bible is not explicit as to what David *felt* in that moment, but it becomes obvious through his actions that David finds himself that evening in the throes of temptation. He sees the woman, she is naked, and he wants her. And in that moment David sees the woman's nakedness and is desperately tempted to go beyond what he knows is right in the sight of God. But in that moment he hadn't yet taken that first step into sin.

Temptation versus Sin

Let's pause for a second and deal with what David is experiencing in this moment. David is at a critical crossroads—the crossroads of temptation and sin. One of the greatest lessons I've learned over the years is that there is a difference between temptation and sin. Let's take lust for example. To see someone and find her attractive is not a sin; that just means you're human. But if you continue to linger on that person's attractiveness, it can lead to a *temptation* to lust. But it's what you do *after* the temptation comes that determines if the temptation turns into something that falls short of the glory of God.

If, after you see an attractive person, you divert your eyes and mind and heart to what is holy and pure, you've been tempted, but you haven't sinned. But, if in the moment of temptation, you allow your eyes to linger, your mind to wander, or your heart to pursue that temptation, you've taken a step and crossed a line. Temptation has become sin.

The next verse in the story is telling as we clearly see David take that step from temptation to sin. "So David sent and inquired about the woman" (2 Sam. 11:3). Do you see it? He took the step. He took the bait. Temptation came and he plowed right through it.

The writer of the book of James describes the cross-roads of temptation and sin this way: "But each one is tempted when he is carried away and enticed by his own lust. Then when lust has conceived, it gives birth to sin" (James 1:14–15). James teaches us that in the moment we are tempted, we either turn and run to God, *or* we are "carried away and enticed by [our] own lust." In other words, after temptation comes, we "take the step" into sin.

When describing this step, James makes an interesting analogy. He says that when lust (temptation) is conceived, it *"gives birth to sin."* He says that when we cross the line from temptation to sin, it's like a conception of a baby. And what is the inevitable outcome of conception? Something is eventually going to be born. When temptation occurs and that fateful step is taken, the inevitable result is the birth of an ugly, screaming baby called sin. Look one last time at James 1:15:

> Then when lust has conceived, it gives
> birth to sin; and when sin is accomplished,
> *it brings forth death.* (emphasis added)

James says that if we're tempted and we take the step, we conceive a sin baby; and when that baby is born, it has a name. It's called death. Friends, here's the point of this Scripture: sin never ends well. Never. Whether you're Adam and Eve in the garden, King David on a roof, or a college kid at a party on a Friday night, taking the step from temptation to sin will result in some pretty devastating consequences.

The rest of the story of King David plays out just as the writer of James says it would. David sleeps with the woman, gets her pregnant, tries to cover his sin by having her husband killed in battle; and that one decision—that one step from temptation to sin—would wreck his life in ways he could never have imagined.

I heard a sermon years ago from a preacher who was teaching on the subject of David's sin. After he told the story, he asked a question, "What if, somehow, a seventy-year-old David could get in a time machine and travel back in time to the roof that night. What would the seventy-year-old David say to the thirty-something David before he chose to sleep with Bathsheba?" The preacher's cadence began to grow quicker, and his voice began to boom. "I *know* what the seventy-year-old David would say to the thirty-year-old David on the roof that night. He would grab that young man by the shoulders, pull him close to his face, and say 'Don't do it, David. Go back into the house! It's not worth it. If you make this decision, it will set into motion a series of events you can never recover from. *Please* David. Go back in the house.'"

Most sermons I have heard throughout my life have moved me toward God in the moment of my hearing them, but few have stuck with me beyond that Sunday. Not so with this sermon. I've thought about it many times over the years as I've stood at the countless crossroads of temptation and sin. And every single time I've chosen to believe the lie and take the step toward sin, it's always ended the same way. Death. Death of purity, death of integrity, death of trust, death of the life abundant that God has promised. And what I wouldn't give to go back in a time machine and grab that eighteen- or twenty-one- or twenty-eight- or thirty-two-year-old Matt by the shoulders and say, "Matt, for goodness' sake, boy. It's not worth it. Go back in the house!" But I can't. Far too many times I have taken that step and had to suffer the consequences of that decision.

Letting the Past Speak to the Present

I want you to stop for a second and think about your past. While some of you reading this book are young, and maybe have never taken a good long trip down the road of sin, others of you have a little more life under your belt and you have. I actually want you to stop reading for a second and think about your biggest mistake—your worst sin.

There, you got it?

Let me ask you a question: How did it turn out for you? If you're honest, was it worth it? Did that temptation that turned into sin deliver what it promised? Or did it leave you hurting and empty?

When I was a teenager, I truly believe I was a Christian, but I most definitely wasn't walking with Jesus. For most of my teenage years, I was a little frumpy—a little overweight and more than a little awkward when it came to my dealings with the opposite sex. Because of that, for most of my high school years, girls didn't pay much attention to me, and I hated it. I had a friend who was really good-looking and in great shape. He was funny and kind and charming, and girls loved him. I watched him with envy have the ability to date any girl he wanted, but for years I was forced to sit on the sidelines and do just that—watch.

Then, in the summer before my senior year, everything changed. As I shared in the previous chapter, I went to work at a kid's summer camp and spent most of my summer working in the grueling Texas heat. In just a couple of weeks, I started noticing a change. The fat in my face and midsection was melting off. I looked in the mirror and saw something I'd never seen before, a jawline. A couple of weeks after that I realized I was actually growing some muscles and was seeing the beginning of the coveted six-pack abs every guy longs for. The physical transformation of my body that summer was pretty profound, and that change in my appearance also led to a big boost in my confidence. So, after that long summer in the sun, when I returned home, I looked and acted like a different guy.

After that fateful night at the Halloween party, the girl I met at summer camp and I broke up, and when the news spread around school, something miraculous happened. Multiple girls started paying attention to me. Girls that I had crushes on for years, but were thoroughly out of my league, were all of a sudden coming up to me and starting conversations, and I ate it up. I started getting invited to parties and began to be included in social circles that I only dreamed of in the previous years. I know, teenagers can be shallow, but I didn't care—girls were interested, and I took full advantage of it.

I remember being at a party and a girl I had always liked started flirting with me. The flirting led to her asking me if I wanted to join her in one of the upstairs bedrooms, and in that moment I knew I was at a crossroads. Was I tempted? You better believe it. This is what I'd always wanted, right? But I had been to church enough to know that if I walked across that line, it would be a sin.

Now, remember what I talked about in the last chapter? How God says one thing but Satan lies to us. God says that the best life has to offer is in purity and obedience to Him. But the lie Satan was whispering to me was that the most fun, the most fulfilling experience I could find was with that girl. I knew the truth, but in that moment I was believing the lie. For crying out loud, it sure sounded fun, so I had to find out for myself. I agreed and I walked into that room.

What I discovered firsthand that night was that what James wrote in the Bible all those years ago was actually true. *When lust is conceived, it gives birth to sin. And when sin is accomplished, it brings forth death.* Did I die that night? Obviously not. But something did die inside of me. I experienced the death of purity, and it ripped my guts out. You see, I was saved, I had the Holy Spirit inside of me, and He was grieved. After I took that step into sin, I was wracked with the guilt that only a child of God experiences when he walks headlong into a sin that caused Jesus to walk to the cross.

On top of that, I was hit with the reality that I would one day have to look my future bride in the eye and tell her about what I did that night, and it tore me apart. I remember sitting on the steps of my front porch that evening, sobbing and heaving with regret. I had been sold a big fat lie, I believed it, took the step, and it produced a death inside of me that I never saw coming.

I want you to know something. I would give just about anything to go back in time and relive that night. If somehow the forty-five-year-old Matt could go back in time and speak to the eighteen-year-old Matt, I would walk right up to him and say, "You are about to make one of the worst decisions of your life." I would tell him the story of the night where he sat down in front of his bride, who was a virgin when she got married, and how I had to tell her that story. I would tell him of the tears streaming down her face and the fear and uncertainty that one sin would put in her heart, the questions of whether I could be trusted to say no to sexual temptation in the future. I would tell him of the times in the years to come, when I said no to those same temptations and how wonderful and life-giving those decisions were. Then I would grab him by the ear, walk him out the door, and tell him to go home and spend time with his mother who would die when he was in his twenties and he would miss her desperately.

Do you have a story like that or at least one similar to it? Most of us do. Let me ask you again, was that sin worth it? Did the sin live up to what it promised? What would the right-now you say to the then you, if you could go back in time and talk? Would you encourage that younger you to go ahead with that sin? Or would you beg your earlier self to turn around and walk away? If you're truly a child of God, of course you would want a different outcome. But unfortunately, when we're at the crossroads of temptation and sin, we get so caught up in the moment that we don't think about the consequences of our actions.

The Great Cloud of Witnesses

The Bible doesn't specify if the story of the prodigal son really happened. It's a parable, so it's entirely possible it's just that, a story. But it's also possible that Jesus told this story because it really occurred. If that's true, and our prodigal was a man who really walked down this road of failure and forgiveness, then we'll see this guy in heaven one day. That's pretty cool if you think about it. One day we'll get to talk to him face-to-face in heaven. Who knows? I guess we'll see.

But one thing for certain is that the Bible teaches us we are right now surrounded by *a great cloud of witnesses*. That's a term the Bible uses to describe the believers who have gone before us and are cheering us on from heaven—rooting for us to keep going and keep walking toward Jesus, even when it's really hard.

The Bible doesn't say who is in our great cloud of witnesses. But one thing to consider is that if this story really happened—and the prodigal was a real man—I like to think that maybe *he* is a part of that faithful crowd cheering me on—and maybe yours too. If he is, and right now you are at the crossroads of temptation and sin, then I have no doubt he's screaming one thing at you from the top of his lungs: "Don't take the step! It's not going to turn out like you hope. I promise you, nothing compares to life with God!" And what we're about to see is that if anyone would know, he would.

The beauty of the story of the prodigal son is that Jesus lets us live vicariously through a young man at that same crossroads. He's heard the lie that there is a better life for him outside of the love of his father. He believed the lie, and he takes that first step down the road that will lead to a lot of death and destruction. For those of us who are right now standing at that same crossroads, the story of the prodigal son lets us see a glimpse into our own future. It allows us to walk down the road alongside this young man without having to take the trip ourselves, all with the hope that we would hear his story and learn from his monumental mistakes. Jesus told this story in the hope that if our own past won't help us make better choices moving forward, maybe his past will.

So if the prodigal's story is your story, and as you are reading this book, you're standing at that same cross-roads where the prodigal stood—the crossroads of temptation and sin—I want you to know I'm praying for you. As I write these words, I'm praying that you will ignore the lying whispers of your enemy and choose to believe the whispers of your Savior: *There is no life in the faraway land. Stay at home. There is life and peace and joy at home. If you're going to take a step, turn around and take a step toward Me.*

For others of you that are reading this, you have already taken the step to the faraway land, and you are wondering if you are beginning to feel the sickening sting of your decisions. I know the questions you are asking yourself: "How did I get here? Can I ever go home? Will my heavenly Father receive me back knowing all that I have done?" I know those questions because I've been where you are, and I've asked them myself. Hang with me. Good news is coming. But before we get there, let's take a little more time to look at what lies ahead of us in the faraway land of sin.

CHAPTER 4

The Consequences

Nobody would ever walk down the road to sin if they knew what lay at the end of the journey. Seriously, think about it. How many men have you seen throw their lives away through an affair and at the end of it all, with their life in ruins, thought to themselves, *Man! That was totally worth it! I'd definitely do that again?*

How many times has that happened?

Exactly never.

Over the years I cannot tell you how many times I've counseled young men and women who walked down the path of sin and heard them say something like, "I had no idea what I was thinking. How did I get to this place? If I had only known what kind of destruction I would bring to my life, I would do things so much differently."

It's an all too common theme: the young man who takes his first drink in junior high only to wake up thirty years later with his life in shambles because of alcoholism. Or the college girl who went to the beach on spring break only to carry the weight and guilt of that week's decisions for the rest of her life. What about the young man who goes too far sexually with his girlfriend, eventually breaks up, and has to share those decisions with his future wife?

I could go on and on, but the theme holds true across the board: nobody would ever walk down the road of sin if they truly knew what lay at the end of their journey.

One of the beautiful aspects of the story of the prodigal son is that we get to stand on the sidelines as he takes that journey, and we get to see the end result without having to travel the road ourselves. So far we've seen the young man believe the lie that there was life outside the love of his father, and he's taken that fateful first step down the path of sin and rebellion. Now let's see what lies ahead for him at the end of the road:

> And not many days later, the younger son
> gathered everything together and went on
> a journey into a distant country, and there
> he squandered his estate with loose liv-
> ing. Now when he had spent everything,
> a severe famine occurred in that country,
> and he began to be impoverished. (Luke
> 15:13–14)

As Jesus tells this young man's story, He wastes no time in telling us of the consequences of the prodigal's decision. The son takes a trip to the faraway land, and in a short time he squanders his inheritance on what Jesus calls "loose living." The word *loose* comes from the Greek word *asotos*, and in the original language it carries with it a much stronger meaning than most English translations. *Asotos* is a word that might be better translated as *riotous*. In other words, Jesus tells us that the young man went to the faraway land and lost his mind. Jesus paints a picture of this guy taking his inheritance and spending it recklessly on every passion, desire, or lust he could get his hands on. Fleshly living is one thing, but riotous living goes to a whole other level. The word carries with it

THE LONG WALK HOME

the idea of partying, drunkenness, and prostitutes. Jesus used that word to paint a picture for us that if there was something or someone or some experience he wanted, he went for it.

At this point in the story, I think the young man's actions beg the question, "Was the world and all its pleasures everything he had always hoped? Was his decision to go all-in for a life of sin everything he thought it would be? *And was there really a better life waiting for him in the faraway land?*" Jesus answers those questions with a resounding no.

> Now when he had spent everything, a severe famine occurred in that country, and he began to be impoverished. So he went and hired himself out to one of the citizens of that country, and he sent him into his fields to feed swine. And he would have gladly filled his stomach with the pods that the swine were eating, and no one was giving anything to him. (Luke 15:14–16)

Jesus wastes no time in letting us know whether the young man found a better life apart from the love of his father. Jesus tells us, "When he had spent everything, . . . he began to be impoverished." Through this one little statement, Jesus gives us some incredible insight into the nature of sin and its impact on the life of a child of God. Through the words of Jesus and through the eyes of the prodigal son, we learn vicariously one of life's most essential lessons:

> *For the child of God, sin always equals poverty.*

Jesus shared this part of the story to show us once and for all that sin is a dead-end road, with the final destination being the stinking mud of a pigpen. This young man took the journey to the faraway land hoping to find fun and joy and the fullness of life, but when the party was over, he woke up broke, hungry, and covered in slop.

As I shared earlier in the book, believing a lie is the beginning of every sin. Our enemy, the father of lies, continually tries to deceive us into believing that obedience to God will result in our missing out on the best life has to offer. He loves to whisper to us that sexual purity is outdated and that a single man or woman, saving themselves for marriage, is truly missing out on one of life's most pleasurable experiences. Satan loves to convince us that putting our family and marriage on the back burner in order to pursue the pleasures of money and financial security is a better path than a simple life of contentment.

Our enemy is truly skilled at trying to get us to buy the lie that service to God and His church just doesn't compare to weekends at the lake house with our friends. He's truly proficient at making young wives believe their husband will never fill their deepest longings for love, but that other guy at the office just might.

Fill in a different whispered lie in your own life, but the stories the enemy tells us always have the same theme: obedience to God equals boredom and lifelessness; but sin equals fun, excitement, and true happiness. Through the story of the prodigal son, Jesus is shouting from the rooftops for us to see those things for what they really are—lies.

The Beautiful Mirage of Excess

Over and over again throughout the entirety of Scripture, the Bible makes a radical claim: the fullest and most satisfying expression of life can only be found in obedience to God. But too often the burning questions that lie just below the surface of our hearts is: Can that really be true? How in the world can *the best* life has to offer be found in following the guidelines of a book written thousands of years ago? As a man who has taken a few trips down the path of sin, I can honestly tell you that the claim of Scripture is 100-percent true. But before I explain that further, let's take a second and talk about *why* sin *never* delivers what it promises.

There is an interesting book in the Bible called Ecclesiastes. If you forced me to come up with a thesis for its content, I would probably say something like this: "All of life is vanity." The book, historically believed to have been written by King Solomon, is a simple tale of one man's quest for ultimate happiness. As the book unfolds, we see King Solomon, a man of untold wealth and privilege, go on a journey to discover if real happiness can be found in the stuff the world has to offer. Because of

Solomon's limitless wealth and power, he found himself in the unique position to see for himself if the stuff of the world can live up to the hype.

Imagine for a second that you're a billionaire, and not just an ordinary billionaire, but there is literally no end to your money. So vast is your wealth that you could spend and spend and spend, and the money would never run out. What would you buy? What would you experience? Imagine also that you had inexhaustible power—and not the kind of power of a typical United States president, but the power of an ancient king—with an entire kingdom ready to respond to your every whim. Sounds pretty cool, huh? This is our man Solomon. If the world offered it, he had the capacity to experience it. And he did, all in pursuit of what could bring him ultimate happiness.

Throughout the book he gives us a list of all the world's pleasures he indulged in trying to find happiness. He tried sex. He slept with literally hundreds of women. Any woman he saw who captured his attention, he took her for himself. He accumulated material possessions. He bought houses and cars (chariots), good food, wine, and expensive clothes. Everything and everyone his heart desired—he took it.

He also tried to find happiness in his work. He threw himself headlong into the projects he thought might give him meaning and fulfillment. He even tried finding happiness through the acquiring of knowledge and wisdom. He claimed to have gathered more knowledge than anyone who had gone before him in Jerusalem. Like a kid in a candy story, he moved from one experience to the next, on and on and on—but the end result of every one of these pursuits was the same. Interestingly, King Soloman said, "They were vanity." He described each attempt at finding happiness in the stuff of the world as "chasing after the wind." Honestly, I love that description. Have you ever tried to chase after the wind? Not easy to do. No matter how hard you try, you'll never catch it.

Women, cars, houses, sex, power, money, fulfilling work—aren't those things *the best* reasons for living? Aren't those the marks and finish lines of a successful life? Not according to the guy who was once the richest and most powerful man in the world. King Solomon went on a lifelong journey of pursuing happiness through worldly experience only to discover that what the world thinks is the best life has to offer is at most a mirage—a vision of something beautiful and fulfilling that once it has been experienced proves empty and unsatisfying. Every single time.

The whole point of the book of Ecclesiastes is the claim that nothing in all of the world can meet and satisfy the deepest longings of the human heart. And if the claims of Solomon are true, and they are, then here is a really important question: Why does the best the world has to offer never produce in us the happiness that every heart deeply longs for? Solomon gives us the answer in Ecclesiastes 3:11:

> He has made everything beautiful in its time. Also, he has *put eternity into man's heart*, yet so that he cannot find out what God has done from the beginning to the end. (ESV, emphasis added)

What the Bible just said is that God put *eternity* in your heart. What does that mean? It means that God has placed a longing inside of every one of us for the eternal. The next part of the verse describes to us the implications of that eternal longing. Scripture says, "So that [man] cannot find out what God has done from the beginning to the end." That's a really fancy way of saying that because God put an eternal hunger inside of you, you simply cannot satisfy that *eternal* hunger with the *temporal* stuff of the world—from the beginning to the end of your life. The bad news of Ecclesiastes 3:11 is that absolutely *nothing* in this whole world will ever satisfy the hunger inside you because that hunger is not a worldly hunger; it's an eternal one.

Will you stop for a second and think about this eternal hunger God said He put in your heart? Maybe you've never thought about it, but you've probably become aware of those hungers and just didn't realize it at the time. Have you ever sat on the side of a really tall mountain and got quiet long enough to soak in the beauty and majesty of the countless miles of expanse before you? What did you experience in that moment? How did you feel? What did the unimaginable beauty of that moment stir in your heart?

What about the times when you've sat on a beach and seen a sunset that was painted in indescribable colors of orange, red, and hues of purple from horizon to horizon? Think for a second about how you *felt* in those moments? What did those pictures of transcendent beauty produce inside of you?

For me, in those moments where I have encountered the indescribable beauty and majesty of creation, I've noticed an interesting response in my heart. My expectation was that those things would produce in my soul a deep sense of satisfaction—but time and again I've noticed that actually the opposite occurs. Those experiences don't produce in me a profound sense of satisfaction but rather a profound sense of longing. The best way to describe how I feel when I see the beauty of a sunset is homesickness. The best way I can describe the way I feel when I see the majesty of the Rocky Mountains or the turquoise waters of the Caribbean is that it produces in me a hunger for even more majesty. I've noticed that transcendent beauty doesn't deeply satisfy me, but instead it uncovers in my soul a realization that I was created for a greater and more transcendent beauty who this world can never offer.

Where does that longing and homesickness come from? The Bible tells us: God placed eternity in the heart of man. Why did He place that eternal longing in you? So that you might turn to Him, the eternal God of the universe, and be satisfied. Think about it: in the garden of Eden, man and woman walked in the cool of the day, experiencing the unfathomable beauty and majesty of their Creator face-to-face. But sin entered into the picture, and we lost our ability to daily encounter the eternal beauty of God. And so now, when we encounter little micro glimpses of beauty and majesty here on Earth, it exposes that eternal hunger God placed in all of our hearts, meant to be met and satisfied in Him.

A few years ago I experienced another example of this eternal hunger in the hearts of men through a friendship I developed with a famous football player. Back in 2008, I became friends with a young man named Colt McCoy. For those of you who don't know him, Colt was a four-year starter and quarterback for The University of Texas. At the end of his senior year, Colt McCoy had won more football games than any quarterback in the history of college football.

Because of his success, especially in Austin, Colt became somewhat of a legend. Not only did he have one of the coolest quarterback names ever, but he had brought to the Longhorn Nation what they want more than anything—victories (and a lot of them). He was the hero of every little (and grown-up) boy in Texas, and everywhere he went people recognized him.

During his time at UT, Colt began to attend my church. I'd see him walk in on Sunday evenings with twenty or so of his teammates following behind him. The masses of people standing in the hallways of the church would stop and stand in awe as these giants of the gridiron came walking into the sanctuary to worship. At the beginning of his senior year, Colt approached me about the possibility of mentoring him. He explained that the pressure of his senior season was immense (he was favored for the Heisman Trophy, and the Longhorns were poised for a national championship run), and he felt that some wise counsel and mentoring would serve him well throughout the season-long pressure cooker that is UT football. We met once a week, prayed, read Scripture, and talked about what it looked like to be a man of God in such a difficult environment.

As the years have gone by, what began as a mentorship has formed into a friendship of peers, and I've had the privilege of spending hours upon hours sharing life with this man and realizing that he's exactly that—just a man. Yes, Colt McCoy has a unique ability. He can throw a football better than all but a handful of people who walk the planet. But at the end of the day, he's just a normal human being like you and me. The world knows him as Colt McCoy the legendary UT quarterback. But I know Colt McCoy the man, the dad, the husband, and the friend. To me he's just another buddy of mine.

Shortly after I met him, I realized that because of who he is and what he's accomplished, the average person viewed him in a radically different way than I did. We'd be at dinner and people would walk by, see him, and literally stop in their tracks. They would stand in awe and mumble incoherently something to the effect of, "You're Colt McCoy." Still others were not very subtle in their response to spotting him. We'd sit at dinner, and shortly after the first person recognized him, a line would begin to form. People wanted to talk to him, get his autograph, or take a picture to post on social media. I've seen grown men absolutely lose their mind and start freaking out like a teenage girl at a Justin Bieber concert when they were in his presence.

Here's a question for you: Why in the world do people respond to him that way? And here's another question: Why do people not respond that way to you?

Since I met Colt, people's response to him has always fascinated me. Why do people encounter someone famous and lose their ever-loving minds? And here is the only explanation I can come up with: we were *created* to encounter, to be in relationship with and *worship* the most famous "person" in all of the universe—God. Their response is as natural as breathing air because we were literally created to worship the King of kings and the Lord of lords. And in the garden of Eden, before sin entered into the picture, that's exactly what we did.

But what happened? The first humans sinned, and because of their sin, we lost the ability to have face-to-face encounters and relationship the "famous One."

What is the result? Because we were created to worship and be in relationship with the epitome of fame and power—but lost it—that loss has put inside of us a longing to encounter the greatness we once experienced with God.

So now, when a normal, everyday person walks past a table in Chuy's Mexican restaurant and sees somebody famous, that eternal longing comes bubbling to the surface, and that person does everything possible to encounter them. They desperately want to connect, to talk, to engage with this person of fame. I can think of no better explanation to this phenomenon than that the words of Ecclesiastes are true: "God set eternity in the hearts of men." And unfortunately, most people will spend their whole lives trying to fill those longings with people, places, and things that simply do not have the ability to fulfill them.

The Most Miserable Person in the World

In light of the reality that God has placed eternity in the hearts of man, I'd like to raise one final question: How does this truth impact *Christians* who try to fill their eternal longings with the stuff of the world? What are the consequences when we choose the stuff of the world over God to fill our eternal longings? We've already discussed how this affects nonbelievers: they try to meet those longings with the stuff of the world, and it simply doesn't work. But what happens when a *Christian* makes that same choice? I want to begin to answer that question by making a bold claim: a Christian who is walking in unrepentant sin is the most miserable person in the world. Now make no mistake—when a nonbeliever sins, it definitely will lead to misery. But the point I'm trying to make is that the effects of sin on a believer are more consequential.

Let me explain by describing what happens when believers turn to the Lord (the Eternal One) to meet the deepest needs of their heart (eternal longings). The answer is pretty simple. They are satisfied. If I've learned anything in my forty-five years of life, I've learned that one Person, and one Person alone, can actually meet and satisfy those eternal longings. And that person is Jesus.

When I'm alone in study, pouring over His Word; when I am standing on the front row of my church, hands in the air, singing at the top of my lungs; when I'm on my knees in prayer, feeling and experiencing the tangible, real, all-encompassing presence of God, I've found that there is simply nothing like it in the world. The words of the psalmist have, for me, proven true time and time again: "In Your presence is fullness of joy" (Ps. 16:11). There is no peace like the peace God gives. There is no joy like the joy God gives. There is no more profound sense of safety or pleasure than I feel when I am walking with my Lord and Savior.

Jesus described this reality in the Beatitudes when He said, "Blessed are the pure in heart, for they shall see God" (Matt. 5:8). When you look deeply at those words, you realize that Jesus is making a pretty radical statement. First, He begins the sentence with the word "Blessed." The specific Greek word Jesus uses carries with it the idea of the fullest expression of blessing and happiness a person can experience. What produces this radical happiness and blessing? Jesus says when our hearts are pure. The word *pure* means "unmixed or undivided." So what Jesus is conveying is that Christians can experience the greatest level of happiness when their hearts are fully devoted to God and not divided by God and something else. And why is the Christian with an undivided heart so blessed? Jesus says, "They shall see God.

The word *see* is key in understanding what Jesus is talking about. He's not claiming that when our hearts are pure we'll literally see the face of God, but rather it's a word that means "to experience to the point of producing awe." Jesus is teaching us that when our are hearts are unmixed, we experience the highest form of human happiness because we experience the presence of God to the fullest. On the other hand, when our hearts are divided and we give part of our heart to some other person or possession, that hinders and muddies our experience of God's presence. So if the fullness of joy is found in God's presence, if you have a divided heart, you simply cannot experience that fullness.

Are you beginning to see why I say, that a Christian walking in sin is the most miserable person in the world? Sin makes your heart "mixed" and keeps you from meeting the deepest longings of your heart in the presence of the Lord. But the consequences don't stop there.

There's another interesting result of a divided heart. It grieves the Holy Spirit. The Bible teaches us that at our salvation the Holy Spirit (God) takes up residence in our hearts. And here's the thing you need to understand about the Holy Spirit who lives in you. He hates sin. It's totally contrary to His nature, so now that He lives in you, He won't leave you alone until you repent of that sin. The result? If you're a Christian, you no longer have the ability to enjoy sin. You might for a minute, but that grieving of the Holy Spirit won't let you enjoy it for long. Does a nonbeliever's sin produce misery? Yes. But because of the Holy Spirit, the misery of a believer's sin goes to a whole other level.

Let's look one last time at how Jesus describes the consequences of the prodigal son's rebellion:

> Now when he had spent everything, a severe famine occurred in that country, and he began to be impoverished. (Luke 15:14)

When Jesus tells us the prodigal was impoverished, He wasn't just talking about physical poverty but spiritual poverty as well. When the son turned his back on his father and took a trip to the faraway land of sin, he didn't just wreck his life; he wrecked his soul. He discovered firsthand the harsh reality that everything he thought would bring him joy actually brought him pain, misery, and guilt. But there's a silver lining in all this young man's suffering. *His pain would be the catalyst he needed to wake him up and make him start his journey home.*

You see, the bad news for the believer walking in sin is that it will produce emptiness and misery every single time. But the good news is that when a believer sins, the Holy Spirit will use that emptiness and misery to serve as a reminder that there is a place, and a home, and a Person that will always take you back, restore you to wholeness, and fill the deepest longings of your heart.

Some of you may be in that place today, and I want you to know something. That emptiness you feel because of your sin is the kindness of God, gently calling you home. Make no mistake, sin and its consequences are profound. But even in the midst of your sin, God is still at work. Sin's inability to satisfy your deepest longings is nothing more than the tender and beautiful whisper of God that there's more to this life than what you're experiencing. Ask God to help you see sin for what it is—vanity, and I promise you He will. But before you can go home—just like we'll see the prodigal son do next—you have to come to your senses, stand up, and walk out of the pigpen.

CHAPTER 5

The Realization

Coming to Your Senses

We come to a place in the story of the prodigal son that is one of my favorite verses in all the Bible. I've used it many times throughout my time as a pastor—in counseling, in preaching, and when I personally needed to be reminded that sin is never a wise or acceptable path for the child of God. The part of the story I'm referring to is when the prodigal finds himself in a pigpen. This young man has fallen about as far as a person can fall. He's abandoned his family, spent all of his inheritance on parties and prostitutes, and now finds himself in the worst situation of his entire life. A famine has come into the "faraway land," and he finds himself starving, dirty, with all his money gone; and the shame of what he's done begins to set in. In other words, he's hit the proverbial rock bottom.

We discussed in the previous chapters that sin, by its very nature, is deceiving. On the front end sin almost always looks enticing, pleasurable, good, fun, and exciting. But the problem with sin, at the end of the day, is that it never delivers what it promises. And the prodigal has just learned this lesson the hard way. Everything he thought would bring him happiness has actually produced a pain and misery he never could've imagined. We also talked about how God, in His goodness, lovingly uses that misery to gently call us home. What we're about to see is that the pain and suffering the prodigal is going through actually serve as a wake-up call to bring him back to the father he never should have left.

God's Relentless Pursuit of Us *through* Our Sin

Have you ever wondered why God allows His children to sin in the first place? I have wrestled with that question many times throughout my life. On the other side of sin, sitting in the pigpen of shame and misery, I've found myself crying out to God, "Why did You let me go here in the first place?" It's a valid question. God's is all-knowing and all-powerful, right? At any point, when his sons and daughters are standing at the crossroads of temptation and sin, He could intervene, maybe write something in the clouds along the lines of: "Stop, you idiot. You are about to make a monumental mistake—God."

But He doesn't.

Even though every bad decision in my life can be squarely placed in my lap, I have often found myself being tempted to think that God was somehow cruel or uncaring in allowing me to succumb to my temptations. But I have found something interesting about how God works in regard to His kids—sometimes it takes us tasting the bitter fruit of sin for us to fully realize the sweetness of God's love.

Now, I am in no way advocating sinning to fully experience God's grace. The apostle Paul has some pretty strong words about that course of action, but what I am saying is that for the true child of God, a special grace comes to us, even in the midst of our sin.

What happens next in our story serves as a beautiful picture of this special grace:

> But when he came to his senses, he said, "How many of my father's hired men have more than enough bread, but I am dying here with hunger!" (Luke 15:17)

Our boy is in the pigpen, hurting, stinking, and sin sick. And then he has a revelation.

Jesus tells us that "he came to his senses." The young man asks himself, "How many of my father's hired men have more than enough bread, but I am dying here of hunger!" In this very moment the prodigal son realizes he had been profoundly wrong in his opinion of his father's house. Remember the lie he believed at the beginning of the story? "There is a better life for me outside of my father's house." Sitting there in the slop of his sin, it hits him like a lightning bolt that he was dead wrong. He had made a grave mistake. The young man had learned the hard way that life, in fact, was NOT better in the faraway land.

Have you ever found yourself in a moment like that? If you're a Christian, and you live long enough, you probably will. Maybe you looked at pornography, because, hey, you were tired or bored or just plain curious, but afterward you were left with the stinging realization that your sin didn't deliver what it promised. Maybe you were being pressured by a boyfriend to go farther sexually than you knew to be right. And in the moment, you thought to yourself, *I'm tired of waiting, tired of being thought of as a prude. I really think I want to do this,* only to find yourself, afterward, wracked with guilt and shame and anger that only comes on the other side of being used.

We've all been there in some capacity, and what I've come to realize over the years is that when it comes to His sons and daughters, while God may let us take a trip to the faraway land, He never lets us *stay* there, not forever. The apostle Paul wrote about this special grace of God in the midst of our sin:

> For I am confident of this very thing, that He who began a good work in you will perfect it until the day of Christ Jesus. (Phil. 1:6)

That verse is at once one of the most comforting and scariest verses in all of Scripture. Paul begins the statement like this: "I am confident of this." He essentially lets us know, "Hey, you can take what I'm about to say to the bank." He continues by telling us that the same God who *began* the work of salvation in us will 100 percent, absolutely, positively finish the work He began until the day He comes to take us home. In other words, God always finishes what He starts, and so from the moment of your salvation to the moment you breathe your last breath, God is dead set on keeping you near to Him.

And yes, in one sense that is profoundly comforting. Paul's words promise us that if you are truly His son or daughter He will never let you go. Ever. This verse promises us that if you have walked down the path of sin, there are better, brighter, and holier days ahead of you. And while knowing that God always finishes in you what He began is profoundly comforting, it is also a word of dire warning—a warning that if we are in sin, it ought to cause us to shake in our boots.

I say that because this verse teaches us that God will never sit idly by while his sons and daughters walk down the path of sin. Is He patient when we sin? Yes, more so than our wildest imagination. When His kids walk down the road of sin, He waits and woos and beckons us. But the rebellious child of God must never forget, and hear me clearly here, that there is a limit to His patience. God simply won't allow His children to continue down the broad road that leads to destruction forever. And when we continue in our sin, in His great love He will come at us like a steamroller to bring us back home to Him. As a matter of fact, one of the best evidences that you are a child of God is not that you never sin but that you never continue in your sin. Why?

God promises us He simply won't allow it.

God's Two Ways of Bringing His Children Home

This loving pursuit of God, even in the midst of my own sin, is one of the primary reasons I believe God exists in the first place. At the end of the day, it's why I wrote this book. Every other book that I've published, I've had a coauthor. I love writing with other people, and honestly, I'm just not that good of a writer, so collaboration has served me well. But this book is different. I chose to write a book on the prodigal son by myself because, at the end of the day, his story is my story.

I'm a pastor, and people think I'm supposed to have it all together, but I don't (and I never have). Do I love Jesus? Yes, desperately. He's my dearest friend and the love of my life, but I can't tell you how many times I've walked the road of the prodigal. And every single time I have "made my bed in Sheol" as King David said, "He was there" (see Ps. 139:8). My story is of a man who has far too many times run from God. But mine is also of a story of a God who won't let me go, not for long anyway.

You see, every single time I've walked down the path of sin, one of two things inevitably occur. The first is that the Holy Spirit immediately begins to whisper, "That's not who you are. You were not created for this. Turn around. Come back home." And most times I listen. I head the pleadings of the Spirit that lives within me, and I turn from my sin. But on the handful of occasions I ignored the whisperings of the Spirit and I continue down the path of sin, God brings discipline in my life that inevitably leaves me no option but to come back home. This has been my story. Every. Single. Time. Why?

Because God promises He will discipline those *that He loves.* And whom does He love? He loves His sons and daughters. So the only explanation I have for this dogged, never-ending, relentless pursuit of my holiness, is that I am His son, and He loves me too much to let me continue in my sin.

My "Coming to My Senses" Story

I was born and raised in a Christian home. As my mom used to say, "I was going to church since nine months before I was born." I was eight years old when I remember hearing the gospel for the first time. I was attending a summer day camp at my church called "Camp Sonshine," and I remember it being a blast.

A couple hundred kids would meet every morning at our church and then spend the day swimming, playing games, and doing arts and crafts. After the day's activities we would meet in the fellowship hall to sing songs and listen to a message given by our children's pastor. I don't remember his last name because we simply called him "Brother Jim."

· Brother Jim was a good and a kind man, and I loved him. I'm sure he gave us dozens of talks throughout my childhood, but there was one in particular that would change my life forever. He stood in front of us on that day with a big vase of clear liquid. He raised the vase in the air and spoke to us about how this was the condition of our hearts before sin entered the picture—pure and clear. Then he explained to us that in the beginning of the world, Adam and Eve sinned and chose to disobey God. As he spoke, Brother Jim squeezed a couple of drops of some liquid into the water and, through a cool trick of chemistry, instantly turned the clear liquid to a deep black. He explained that this blackness represented the condition of our hearts because of our sin—black and darkened to the things of God. Then he began to talk about Jesus. He spoke of how sin kept us from a relationship with God and how God loved us too much to stay that way. He shared that God sent Jesus to earth and how Jesus lived a sinless life and shed His blood on the cross to pay the penalty of our sin so we could be reconciled to God. After he spoke of Jesus' death, Brother Jim put a couple of drops of another liquid into the vase. The color of the liquid instantly turned from black to red. He taught us that God changes our darkened hearts by covering them with the blood of Jesus, taking away the blackness of our sin forever.

In the final part of his presentation, Jim took a dropper of liquid and put a few final drops into the vase now filled with a bright red substance. The liquid instantly turned clear again—just like it had been in the beginning. Loud gasps filled the room as every kid in the place was mesmerized by the trick Brother Jim had accomplished, changing the water from clear, to black, to red, then to clear again. Several kids starting shouting out, "How did you do that?" (It's a good question. I'm sure it was a chemistry trick I need to figure out if I ever need to teach to a group of children.) He held the clear liquid up for us to see and explained that this is what happens to our hearts when the blood of Jesus covers us. We're made clear and pure in the sight of God, just as we were created to be. Every child in the room sat there, jaws wide open, in pure awe of what they had seen—every kid but me.

Something besides the creativity of the illustration had captured my attention and my heart. More than the "magic" of the changing colors of the liquid, the story of Jesus blew me away. I had heard the gospel for the first time, and it was messing me up. Even as a middle-aged man, I can still remember what I felt in that moment. My heart was beating fast and tears welled up in my eyes because I couldn't believe God loved me enough to send His own Son to die in my place and make me clean.

Brother Jim asked us to bow our heads and raise our hands if we wanted to ask Jesus to be our Lord and Savior and do in our hearts what he had shown us through the liquid. I instantly raised my hand. Even as an eight-year-old boy, everything within me believed what I had been told, and in that moment I wanted Jesus more than anything in the world.

That day began for me what has become a lifelong relationship with Jesus. From that moment, Jesus has been my best friend and the love of my life. But like many kids raised in church, I didn't always follow Him the way that I should.

In high school I got caught up in a desire for popularity, and in a small East Texas town, being an ardent follower of Christ wasn't the way to achieve those goals.

When I entered college, I stopped attending church. My mother wasn't there to wake me up on Sunday morning, and sleeping in proved a much more appealing activity than attending a worship service. That first semester at Texas A&M, like the prodigal son, was my first real, extended trip to the faraway land. I wanted to find out for myself if there was a better life for me outside of the love of my heavenly Father.

With the restraints of my parents and church behind me, I pretty much went, as they say in East Texas, "wheels off" and did whatever I wanted to do. This was my semester of what Jesus called "riotous living." And on more than one occasion, I fell into sin and got a first-hand experience of what it feels like for a child of God to deliberately disobey God. During that season I allowed the guilt and shame of my sin not to draw me closer to God but instead to push me farther away from Him, and the last thing I wanted to do was go to church and be reminded of how much of a failure I was. And looking back, I was miserable. I wouldn't have admitted it at the time, but I was miserable. I was discovering firsthand the hard lessons the prodigal learned in the pigpen.

Toward the end of the semester, I got a phone call from an old girlfriend in high school, and she invited me to go with her church college ministry on a Christmas break ski trip. Even though I didn't know a single person on the trip (besides her), I reluctantly said yes. The college group was from small towns in the Texas panhandle, and so I met her in Dallas, and we drove up together. As we drove, our relationship was rekindled, and I found myself falling for her again. For the first time in months, I was feeling a sense of happiness. I thought to myself, *Maybe this is what I've been missing? Maybe a real relationship with a girl is what I need to make me happy.*

Well, those hopes were quickly dashed when on day two of the ski trip she informed me that she had met a guy and wanted to ski with him and not me. So there I was, in Colorado, bald (from my freshman year Corps of Cadet haircut) and all alone on the side of a mountain watching my ex-girlfriend ski with another guy. Needless to say, the misery returned in full force.

On the afternoon of the final day, I was sitting by myself in the coffee shop at the base of the mountain when a young man walked up to me. His name was

Brett. Brett was a part of the college group I had come to the mountains with. He recognized me and introduced himself. He asked why I was alone, and I told him how I had been booted to the curb by my now two-time ex-girlfriend. He laughed and asked me if I wanted to ski with him. I did, and through our time together we developed a friendship.

I discovered that he too was a Texas Aggie and that he was a Christian. He asked where I went to church back at A&M. I was honest with him that I hadn't darkened the doors of a church my entire first semester. He told me that he attended a Bible study at A&M and that if I'd give him my number, when we got back to school, he'd call me and we could go together. I gave him my number, never expecting to hear from him again.

I returned to school in January and got back into my same routine, running from God and miserable as ever. On the first Tuesday of the semester, I was in my dorm room studying when my phone rang. It was Brett. He asked me if I wanted to go with him to the Bible study he told me about in Colorado. I didn't, but I didn't want to be mean to this guy who had showed me so much kindness. He picked me up that night, and we drove together to a small chapel in the middle of campus. We walked in the doors together and sat in the back. In the front of the room, there was a college student on a small stage with a guitar. He began to speak and explain that we were going to worship God together. He told us that we had the freedom to sit or stand—to raise our hands or sit quietly and listen. As the song began, I saw something unfold that I had never seen in my eighteen years of attending my small Baptist church in East Texas. College-age kids actually began to worship. I looked around, and every student in the room was singing. Many had their hands raised in the air as they sang. Some even left the rows of chairs and kneeled on the floor as they sang.

I still remember the song the leader was singing that night. He sang the words, "Lord, You are more precious than silver; Lord, You are more costly than gold; Lord, You are more beautiful than diamonds; And nothing I desire compares with You." As the second verse began, I did something that even though I had been in church my whole life I had never done: I began to sing *to* God. Many times in my life I had attended church and sung *about*

God, but I had never truly sung words directly to Him. I closed my eyes and sang, almost in a whisper, these words to Him: "Lord, You are more precious than silver; Lord, You are more costly than gold; Lord, You are more beautiful than diamonds; And nothing I desire compares to You." As I sang, a feeling of warmth and love came flooding over me. Almost instantly the shame and guilt of my sin disappeared as I was engulfed in the presence of this God who had captured my heart as a little boy.

Tears started streaming down my face as I felt the love and forgiveness of God pour into my heart. Barely able to get the words out of my mouth because of my tears, I felt a hand on my shoulder. Brett leaned in and asked me if I was okay. I remember looking at him and said these words: "I've been looking for this my entire life."

I discovered something that night. Jesus alone was able to fill the void in my heart that I had been desperately trying to fill with the stuff of the world. As I turned back and began to sing again, I remember whispering a prayer. I said quietly to God, "Lord, I want to follow You the rest of my life." In that moment I began to walk with

Him, and though I've failed Him many times since, I have never been the same.

I think that brings us to some important questions. What happened to me that night? Why the sudden change of heart? Was I simply caught up in the emotion of the moment? Was God, for me on that night, a crutch that a miserable young man was finally able to lean on?

Yes, it was emotional. And yes, I desperately needed a crutch to prop up my tired and weary soul, but something deeper and more profound was occurring in me in that night. I was a child of God hopelessly trapped in the chains of my sin. But on that cold night in a small chapel in the middle of College Station, Texas, *I came to my senses.* I realized deep within my soul that the place I had found myself was a stinking, empty, and lifeless pigpen of my sin. I realized in that moment that the pigpen was not my home and it never would be. God was my home, and it was time to return to Him.

The Words of Life

A story in Scripture encompasses what I experienced that night. For a period of time in Jesus' early ministry,

He was extremely popular. He was being followed by thousands because He was feeding and healing them, so everywhere He went people wanted to be near Him. Sensing the shallowness of their devotion, Jesus turned to the crowd and exclaimed, "Unless you eat my flesh and drink my blood, you can have no part of me" (see John 6:53). The crowd of thousands, who moments before had been following Jesus, got offended, turned around, and walked away. Everyone left Jesus—everyone but the twelve disciples. Jesus turned to them and asked them a question, "Are you going to leave me too?" Peter replied, "Jesus, where are we going to go? You alone have the words of life" (see vv. 67–68).

From that moment in that chapel in January 1993, I've found those words to be true. Trust me, I've tried it a thousand times, and nothing—and I mean *nothing*—has given me a real sense of lasting joy and peace but the person of Jesus. If Jesus were to ask me if I was going to leave Him, through experience I know what I'd say: "Where am I going to go? You alone have the words of life."

I want to end this chapter by speaking to two groups of people. The first group of people I want to speak to are the ones who are still at home with the Father but are seriously considering taking a trip to the faraway land. Maybe you're wondering, deep down inside in places you don't like to talk about, if you are missing out on the best life has to offer because of your call to follow Christ. I can tell you from firsthand experience, those whispering questions are a lie from the pit of hell. They are whispers of an enemy whose oldest trick is to get you to doubt the promises of your heavenly Father. And he's whispering them for one reason: to kill, to steal, and to destroy.

So you have a choice. You can believe the words of God, or you can take the trip. But remember, at best you will be monumentally wasting your time. At worst, you'll be making the greatest mistake of your life. Please remember that if you are His child, He'll let you take the trip, but a day will always come when like the prodigal son, and me, you will come to your senses and come back home. But unfortunately you'll come home with pig stink on your clothes. It's simply not worth it. Jesus is asking you today, "Are you going to leave me too?" I pray your answer is "Where am I going to go? You alone have the words of life."

Lastly, I want to speak to those of you who are reading this book and are stuck in a pattern of sin. If that's you, I've got some good news and some bad news. The good news is that God will never leave you or forsake you. You might think He has, but I promise you He hasn't. That distance you feel from God is not evidence of His *absence*; it's actually evidence of His *patience*. If there is sin in your life, God has not left you. He is waiting for you to come home. The promises of God are crystal clear; your sin is not more powerful than the love He has for you as His child. He'll *never* give up on you. No matter what.

So the good news is that God will never leave you or forsake you, but here's the bad news: He will never leave you, and He will never forsake you, and that ought to produce in you a healthy amount of fear and trembling. Because if you are in a pattern of unrepentant sin, here's His promise to you: He will move heaven and earth to make sure He completes the work He began in you until the day of Christ Jesus.

So if that is where you find yourself today, put down this book, get on your knees, and cry out to God. First of all, tell Him you love Him, tell Him you miss Him, and tell Him you have come to your senses. Tell Him you are sick and tired of your pigpen of sin and are ready to come home. And as you turn your heart back to Him, never forget that He's waiting there for you. His eyes have never left you. Neither has His love. Sometimes that is really hard to believe, but in the coming pages we'll learn in full just how much He's been longing for your return.

CHAPTER 6

The Speech

*I will arise and go to my father, and I will say
to him, "Father, I have sinned against heaven
and before you. I am no longer worthy to
be called your son. Treat me as one of your
hired servants." (Luke 15:18–19 ESV)*

All children have a story about doing something monumentally stupid and having to face their parents. If you think about it, you probably could come up with several examples from your own life when you broke something, misbehaved, or generally got into trouble and heard the proverbial, "Wait till your dad gets home!" Those hours between the offense and the hour of reckoning can be brutal: Will my dad be merciful, or is he going to kill me? That question haunts the heart of every disobedient child.

Years ago, when my kids were little, my son JD, who was about six at the time, was really getting into baseball. He carried his bat around everywhere, and much to the dismay of his mother, he often swung the bat in the house, not paying the least bit of attention to what or who was near him. He had been warned over and over again to be careful as he was practicing becoming the next Babe Ruth. But as you can imagine, being the overactive six-year-old boy that he was, he didn't listen, and it was only a matter of time before he did some real damage.

One day when I was at work, he and his four-year-old sister Annie were in the backyard playing, and of course, JD had his bat. My wife was inside taking care of our youngest child Sammy, and all of a sudden she heard a bloodcurdling scream coming from my daughter. Annie came running in the house, clutching her mouth as blood streamed between her fingers. JD came running in right behind her, bat in hand, with a look of pure-white terror on his face. He had swung his bat and accidentally hit my daughter with full force, square in the mouth. The blow knocked Annie's front tooth completely out, and she would carry that snaggle-tooth grin with her for the rest of her childhood. My wife, of course, completely lost it. Who wouldn't? Her son, whom she had warned on multiple occasions to be careful with his bat, had just injured his little sister and injured her badly.

Of course, he felt horrible, and while my daughter was crying tears of sheer pain, little JD was crying just as hard out of the deep realization that he had just committed a mortal sin that would probably mean the end of his tender young life. It was a scene of pure chaos, and JD heard the words he knew in his heart would seal his fate. My wife screamed at him, "Wait till your father gets home!"

Since I was at the office, Jennifer called me and through sobs of fear and anger managed to tell me about what happened. I packed up my stuff and headed home to comfort my wife and daughter and deal with my son who had just whacked his sister in the face with a baseball bat. About forty-five minutes later, I walked in the door, and from the hallway I could see little JD sitting on the couch with his head in his hands dreading the moment when he would have to face me.

When he saw me, he immediately jolted from his seated position and stood up on the cushions of the couch and screamed at the top of his lungs, "Dad, it was an accident! I didn't mean to do it! I promise, Dad, I didn't see her. She just walked up behind me and I hit her! Please Dad, I promise you it was an accident!" His pleading screams were so pathetic that my heart instantly melted, and I ran to him, grabbed him into my arms, and started to comfort him. His tears soaked my shirt as I patted his back and told him it was okay and that I knew he didn't mean to do it.

Years later, Jennifer and I have been able to look back on that day and laugh. Annie's permanent tooth eventually grew in, and she has turned out to be an absolute beauty (too pretty for my liking; I prayed that the Lord would make her ugly until college so boys would leave her alone, but the Lord didn't answer my prayer). Even she and JD, who in their teenage years have become incredibly close, look back on that day and laugh. But now one of the things that brings a smile to my face is my poor little JD, standing on the couch, pleading for his life to a dad who he wasn't completely sure wasn't going to murder him.

Looking back, I would imagine that for JD, my forty-five-minute drive between the office and the house was sheer torture. He knew he was in trouble, and he knew the hour of reckoning was about to be at hand. In those long moments before my return, in his sweet, tender little mind, he was *preparing a speech*—a speech he hoped would explain his offense in a way that would melt the heart of his dad and keep him from a punishment he knew might be pretty severe. And it worked. As he delivered his desperate speech to me from the couch, I instantly saw his remorse, and I knew he was truly repentant. JD discovered something that day—a good "I'm sorry" speech can save your life.

In a situation similar to this, we find our prodigal son—except that the offense he committed makes JD's hitting his sister with a bat seem like a trip to Disneyland. You see, at the end of the day, the prodigal son's sin was not the simple act of a childish boy but was one of outright rebellion. His sin was not a one-time act of a careless young man; his sin was a premeditated, thoroughly calculated dagger to the heart of his father. This guy doesn't do your normal, run-of-the-mill kind of sinning; he took a doctoral class in stupidity and graduated with honors. But after the young man wakes up in the pigpen, Jesus tells us that he comes to his senses, realizes the monumental horror of his decisions, and decides to go home. But once the prodigal comes to that conclusion, a realization hits him like a lightning bolt: *I have to face my father.*

I'm sure, as that realization hit him, his heart began beating a little faster, and a hot lump of despair began rising in his throat. How do you come home and face your dad when you have fallen that far? What in the world do you do or say to try to repair the relationship after pulling your father's heart out and ripping it to shreds right in front of him? No doubt these questions and more were echoing in his mind, but regardless, he was dying in the faraway land of sin, and he knew he had no choice but to face the consequences.

Jesus gives us the young man's internal dialogue, and this much is certain: he thinks he's lost the right to be a son. His sin against his father was so grievous that he finds it impossible to imagine waltzing in the front door and things going back to the way they were before. So the young man does the only thing he knows to do. Just like JD on my forty-five-minute ride home, he prepares a speech, a speech he hopes might somehow persuade his father to at least allow him to come home and spend the remainder of his days not as a son but as a hired hand on the family farm.

Now before we look at the prodigal's speech, let me ask you: Have you ever found yourself in a similar situation? Have you ever messed up, sinned, or failed, either in a small or large way, and that sin made you feel a palpable distance between you and God? Sin is weird that way. It creates distance. In the garden of Eden, sin separated Adam and Eve from a relationship with God. But now, because of the cross of Jesus, sin cannot separate us from the love of God, but it can create *a sense* of separation. I experience all kinds of emotions when I sin and fall short of the glory of God: guilt, shame—(those are Satan's favorites by the way) frustration, hopelessness—none of which are good and right. But all those emotions stem from the realization that I let God down *again*. And because I carry around this sense of failure, it sometimes causes me to distance myself emotionally from God, exactly in the moment I should be drawing near to Him.

When I was in college, Jesus won my heart; and unlike my life before Christ, I now wanted more than anything to obey Him. Shortly after my conversion experience, I fell back into a sin pattern that had plagued me before I started walking with Jesus. The main difference was that now I was a Christian. I had the Holy Spirit living inside me, and after I sinned, I was miserable. One of the evidences of a person's salvation is that they begin to hate sin. And man, I hated it. I grieved that particular sin in a way that I had never experienced before. God had transferred me out of darkness into His marvelous light so when I took a detour back into the darkness, it ripped my heart out that I had let God down. I asked God's forgiveness—and in my mind I knew He had—but I couldn't shake that nagging sense of guilt, and I carried it around with me for days.

One of the problems with Sundays is that they come with alarming regularity, and so after I sinned and Sunday morning rolled around, something had changed in my spirit. Normally when the alarm went off on Sunday morning, I would jump out of bed, pumped to be able to go to church and worship God. But this Sunday was different. The memory of my sin was hovering over me like a dark cloud. I began to imagine the guilt and shame I would feel walking into church, so I hit snooze and went back to sleep. When the alarm went off again, somehow I convinced myself to get up and get dressed and go anyway. I knew I needed it, even if I didn't want to be there.

When I walked in the doors and sat down, I looked around and saw everybody talking and smiling. That made things worse. I thought to myself that I was probably the only person in the entire room that was actually a hypocrite. When the first worship song began, it only confirmed my darkest fears.

Everyone else was singing. Everyone else had their hands raised in the air, singing at the top of their lungs with looks of joy and hope covering their faces. Everybody but me. How could I sing to God, knowing what I had just done? How could I just jump back into the routine of worshipping a God I had let down so heinously just a few days before.

Do you see what sin does? It creates a sense of separation, and that's what Satan loves about it. One of the horrible consequences of sin is the distance we suddenly feel between us and God. I was feeling it that morning like I never had before. When I couldn't bear the guilt and shame any longer, I stopped singing, fell back into my chair, and with my hands in my face I gave God my speech: "Father, I'm so sorry. I can't believe I let You down again. After everything You've done for me. After all the ways You have blessed me. I failed You and failed You bad. Please God, please forgive me. Please take me back. I'll never do this ever again."

Have you ever given God a speech like that? You know, the "I've messed up really bad, and I hope that You will not ultimately give up on me" kind of speech? Many of us have. But what we will soon see is that part of my speech was good and appropriate, and part of it was completely unnecessary and actually downright unbiblical. But before we get there, let's take a look at the speech the prodigal hopes will get him back into the good graces of his father.

The Partly Right Forgiveness Speech

In the story of the prodigal son, Jesus tells us that the young man stands up from the pigpen and makes the decision to take the long walk home. But before he takes off, he comes up with a speech—a speech he hopes will somehow repair the relationship with his father enough for him to be allowed back into the house as a hired servant. His speech is simple, only two lines. The interesting thing about the prodigal's speech is that one phrase is right on the money. It's appropriate. It's the kind of thing every one of us should say when we sin and fall short of the glory of God. But unfortunately, in the second sentence of the prodigal's speech, he misses the mark and falls into a familiar trap that so many of us do when we fail to live up to the standard our Father has given us. Let's look at these two lines of the prodigal's speech together because they provide for us some valuable insight into how and why God forgives the sins of His children:

I will arise and go to my father, and I will say to him, "Father, I have sinned against heaven and before you." (Luke 15:18 ESV)

Jesus tells us the young man thinks to himself, "I will arise and go to my father, and I will say to him."

Then, here comes the first line of the speech: "Father, I have sinned against heaven and before you."

The prodigal actually *starts off* his "I'm sorry, Dad," speech with a really appropriate line. You see, when he says, "Father, I have sinned against heaven and before you," those are the words of a truly repentant person. He doesn't start his speech with excuses as to why he sinned. He doesn't start his speech with all the ways the father let him down that led to his leaving in the first place. He doesn't offer any deflection of his failure at all. He just comes right out and owns his sin. He says: "Father, I have sinned against heaven and before you."

Those words are reminiscent of King David's repentance after he committed adultery with Bathsheba and had her husband killed to hide the sin. Look at the words David prays to God:

Wash me thoroughly from my iniquity, and
cleanse me from my sin!
For I know my transgressions, and my sin is
ever before me.
Against you, you only, have I sinned and
done what is evil in your sight,
so that you may be justified in your words
and blameless in your judgment. (Ps.
51:2–4 ESV, emphasis added)

When David realizes the depth of his sin, he doesn't make excuses. He doesn't deflect the blame onto others. He owns 100 percent of the responsibility. David says "For I know *my* transgressions" (emphasis added). Over the years, when dealing with pastoral cases of people falling into sin, I can always tell when a person is truly repentant and when a person is just feeling bad they got caught—and it comes down to this: Do they truly *own* their own sin? Whenever a person caught in sin either downplays their sin or deflects the blame onto other people, I question whether they're truly repentant.

Look at the second thing King David says: "Against you, you only, have I sinned and done what is evil in your sight." Besides truly owning his own sin, David also realizes that first and foremost he has sinned against God. True and genuine repentance always has a horizontal aspect (realizing your sin against others) and a vertical one (realizing you have sinned against God). Realizing you've sinned against another human is important. Realizing you've sinned against the perfectly Holy God of the universe is even more important. He's God, and He's the one that ultimately established the standard of holiness He calls us to live.

Look again at the first line of the prodigal's apology speech, keeping in mind that the father in this story represents God:

> I will arise and go to my father, and I will say to him, "Father, I have sinned against heaven and before you." (Luke 15:18)

"Father, I have sinned." Do you see it? He owns his sin. Then he says, "I have sinned against *heaven and before you*" (emphasis added). His speech has a vertical and a horizontal aspect of repentance. The first line of the young man's speech shows us he's genuinely sorry and shows us a biblically accurate blueprint for how we should respond when we fail.

When we sin, here's what real repentance looks like: First, you own your sin 100 percent. You don't deflect, you don't minimize, and you don't make excuses. You say it's yours and yours alone. Then you demonstrate a knowledge of the primary person affected by your sin—your perfectly holy and righteous heavenly Father. The prodigal does this well: "I have sinned against heaven and before you."

So far so good.

But in the next line of this speech the prodigal son derails, and he derails in a way that is all too common for so many of us:

> "I am no longer worthy to be called your son. Treat me as one of your hired servants." (Luke 15:19 ESV)

This young man is so wracked with guilt and shame over his failure that in the second line of his speech he plans to tell his father that he is no longer worthy to be his son. In the young man's mind his sin is so bad, his failures are so monumental, that he comes to the conclusion he's disqualified himself from sonship. He figures that he's messed up too badly to come back home and pick up where he left off, and so he plans to tell his dad exactly that. "Dad, my sin disqualifies me from being your son. I'm not worthy anymore. So moving forward, if you let me back in the house, I'll no longer be your son, just a hired servant."

This is an interesting part of the story because the young man has fallen prey to another, all-too-common deception of our enemy. Satan loves to tell this lie to the children of God: "Your obedience *qualifies*—and your disobedience *disqualifies*—you as a son or daughter of God." It's one of Satan's most common tactics.

In the beginning of the book, we talked about how the first lie the prodigal believed was that there was a better life for him outside the love of his father. And now, after his trip to the faraway land of sin, we see him believing a second lie that his disobedience can somehow make him lose his standing as a son.

Have you ever fallen prey to this lie? Has there ever been a time in your life where a particular sin or pattern of disobedience keeps appearing in your life and maybe you defeat the sin for a long period, only to succumb to temptation, again, seemingly for the thousandth time?

I know the enemy loves to whisper in our ears in those moments, "Oh! You sinned again!? If you were *really* a son or daughter of God, you would have conquered that sin by now."

Satan really is a punk. He lies to get us to fall into sin. Then after we do, he pounces on us and tells us how much of a failure we are. And the result is we begin to believe those lies and subtly begin to question in our hearts if we really belong to God in the first place.

Two Weapons to Fight the Lies of Satan

Let's take a minute to discuss why we should never allow Satan to have this kind of power over us ever again. There are two realities about our relationship with God that we often forget when we let God down. One is the never-ending love of a good father. And the other is the nature of forgiveness that God offers those who are covered by the blood of Jesus.

Before Jennifer and I had children, I often had people tell me that when I had a child of my own, I would understand the love of my heavenly Father like never before. And you know what? They were right. When Jennifer and I learned she was pregnant with our first son, I instantly loved him.

What's interesting about children is that they're the only people in your life whom you "fall in love with" before you actually meet them. For all three of my children—during the nine months before they were born—I was already desperately in love with these little people I had never even met. I talked to them, sang to them, and prayed over them while they were in their mother's womb. And so when they finally came screaming into the world, it was not only an introduction but a blessed reunion with a beloved child I had already been in relationship with.

The love I felt for my children when I finally saw their faces was fierce and unshakable. I loved them in a way that is hard to put into words. I would do anything for them. I realized in those first moments that I would lay down my life for them without even having to think about it, and I still would. From the first day I realized they had been conceived, I have experienced a depth of affection for my children that is unlike anything I have felt before or since in my entire life.

When my first child, JD, was born, and I finally saw his face, I realized what those people had been telling me was true. As a flawed, earthly father, I realized that if I loved this little guy that much, how much more must my perfect heavenly Father love me? And while seeing JD for the first time most assuredly helped me understand the love of God like never before, the Lord used something else on the day of my son's birth to drive home this reality in a way I never saw coming.

Shortly after JD was born, I was holding him, saying a silent pray over his life and future. I prayed that God would set him apart and use him as a mighty warrior for His kingdom. I remember that as those words came pouring out of my heart, I was overcome with emotion. I started to cry and just stood there with him in my arms, trembling at the incredible depth of love I was experiencing.

As I held him, I felt a hand on my shoulder. I looked up, and *my* dad was standing there beside me. He had come into the delivery room and was seeing his son and firstborn grandson together for the first time. I looked up at my dad, and these words came out of my mouth.

I said, "Dad, I love him so much it hurts."

My dad's response to me in that moment is something I will never forget, and I will share this story at his funeral. My dad looked at me and said, "Son, now you know how I feel about you."

You see, it was one thing for me to realize how much I loved *my* son, but it was something all together different for me to finally realize how much I was loved by my father. I had never fully grasped until that moment that my own father loved me in the same way I loved JD. Right then and there the light finally came on. The love a father has for his children is deep and profound, and I realized God loves me in the same way—and more.

If you don't have children, let me tell you something you might not have fully grasped. If you're a child of God, He loves you more than you can possibly fathom. His love for you is fierce and unshakable. In the same way that there's nothing—and I mean absolutely, positively nothing—that could change how I feel about my children, that is how God loves you. He knew you before you were born, and here's the crazy thing: He was in love with you before you ever came screaming into this world.

The Bible tells us that He chose you to be His son or daughter before you ever lived a day. The Bible also tells us that He ordained for you every day you would live, before you ever lived one. And here's what that means: He even knew all the ways you were going to sin and fail and let Him down. He knew your warts and flaws and hypocrisies long before you ever committed them. And He chose you anyway. God never makes mistakes. He chose you to be His son or daughter, and there is absolutely, positively nothing you have done or ever will do to change the way He feels about you. Not now, not ever.

So when the prodigal son was standing in the pigpen, preparing his speech, he radically underestimated something—the love of a father. The words "I am no longer worthy to be your son" are the words of a person who doesn't understand that our standing as a son or daughter cannot now or ever be lost or minimized or displaced.

Your sin might be fierce, but it's not as fierce as the love your heavenly Father has for you. Some of you need to hear these words—and more important than hearing, you need to believe them. Your sin will never, ever be greater than God's love for you, His child. It's impossibe.

The Radical Forgiveness of God

I recently saw something in Scripture that made me realize I didn't fully understand the forgiveness of God. While I have read and preached thousands of times that because of the blood shed by Jesus on the cross, I am completely forgiven, I recently discovered that I didn't fully comprehend the magnitude of that forgiveness. Not too long ago I studied a verse in 1 John that illuminated in my heart and mind with the depth and breadth of God's forgiveness toward me when I sin. But before I explain it, you need some background on how I used to approach God when I failed Him.

I was exposed to pornography at a young age, and for years it was the sin I kept repeating. And while God has given me incredible victory over that sin, as a young college student who had just begun to walk with Christ, it was a constant temptation for me and one that I periodically fell into. Each time I sinned, I would cry out to God and beg His forgiveness. As I shared earlier, I couldn't understand how, if I was truly a child of God, I could keep falling into a sin I knew was wrong and so detrimental to my heart and walk with Jesus. I remember that each time I failed, I would pray something to the effect of "God, I'm so sorry. Please forgive me. Please have mercy on me." I knew God's mercy was new every morning, and so when I sinned, I would beg for His mercy, hoping against hope that at some point God's mercy toward me wouldn't run out.

But years later, I've realized that not only is it impossible for God to have a mercy limit toward His children, but I also realized that I when I failed, I was praying *the wrong prayer.*

According to 1 John 1:9, "If we confess our sins, he is faithful and just to forgive us our sins and to cleanse us from all unrighteousness" (ESV).

Let's start with the word *confess.* Confession is the role *we* play in regard to God's forgiveness. *Confession* is a word that means to "agree with." In other words, when we sin, we cognitively, emotionally, and verbally agree with God that what we have done is wrong, contrary to His Word, and falls short of His glorious perfection. When I sin, confession looks like I am agreeing in my heart and saying with my mouth to the Lord that what I have done is wrong and contrary to God's best for my life. That's my part, and then God takes it from there.

The next part of the verse is where I was missing the mark in my understanding of God's forgiveness. John writes, "If we confess our sins, he is *faithful* and just to forgive us" (emphasis added). The amazing thing about God is that while we are often unfaithful, He never is. It's impossible for God to be unfaithful to what He promises. So when we confess our sins, there will never be a time or a place or an instance when that sin will cause God to be unfaithful in offering His forgiveness to us. So many of us simply don't believe that reality, and we wonder deep down inside if there's a limit to His forgiveness toward His children. But that could not be farther from the truth! He is faithful—every single time—to forgive you, and there is not a type or quota of sin that can shake or change that faithfulness.

After John tells us that God is faithful to forgive us, he continues and says that God is also *just* to forgive us. This is the part of God's forgiveness that was a new revelation to me. God's *justice* in forgiving sin is a key concept most of us simply haven't thought about. Remember what I prayed when I failed? "God, please be merciful to me!" But notice that the Scripture doesn't say that "when we confess our sins, God is faithful and *merciful* to forgive us"; it says that "God is faithful and *just*" to forgive our sins. Pay attention here because this is incredible.

You see, when Christ came to this earth, He lived a perfect life. He never sinned. And so when God sent Jesus to the cross, He did that so Jesus' shed blood would be the once-and-for-all-time payment for *all* of your sin. Not *part* of your sin. Not *most* of your sin. Not all of your sin except that really bad one you committed in high school. When Jesus shed His blood, it was the complete and total payment for *every* sin you've ever committed and ever will commit.

I love the line from the old hymn, "It Is Well with My Soul." The verse says,

My sin, oh, the bliss of this glorious
    thought—
My sin, not in part, but the whole,
Is nailed to the cross, and I bear it no more,
Praise the Lord, praise the Lord, O my soul!
(emphasis added)[2]

That's it, folks. You can take that to the bank. When Jesus hung on the cross, shed His blood, breathed His last breath, and cried out, "It is finished!," then your sin was exactly that. It was finished forever.

So think about this verse again. When we confess our sins to God, Scripture says God is *just* to forgive us of our sins. Here's what that means: it means that for God *not* to forgive you would be unjust. Why? Because *all* your sin was *already* paid for at Calvary. And for God not to forgive a sin that had already been paid for would be the height of injustice—something God cannot do. Your God is a faithful and just God, and your sin has already and forever been paid for by the precious blood of His Son. His justice *demands* that He never hold that sin against you. Now or forever.

So now when I sin, my prayer is much different.

I pray,

> *God, I confess and agree that what I did was wrong and is contrary to Your nature, and because You are a faithful and just God, I know You have forgiven me. Please help me live my life in light of Your amazing love for me.*

You see the difference? My previous prayer was cloaked in shame, fear, and uncertainty. My new prayer is covered in the confidence of the unshakable love and faithfulness of my heavenly Father who loves me more than my wildest imagination. When we realize that, it changes everything. When we realize we are His sons and daughters and there will never be a sin greater than His faithful and just forgiveness, we are freed not to run from God but to run to God in those times of failure. Owning your sin is a good thing. Guilt and shame are from the enemy. It's one of his most used tactics. If you are a child of God, never let Satan have that power over you ever again.

The First Step on the Long Walk Home

We see that the prodigal has come to his senses. He's realized that he bought the lie that there was love outside of the love of his father and he wants to come home. He has convinced himself that he's failed so badly and fallen so far that he's now unqualified to be a son so he has prepared a speech, hoping that His dad will at least let him come back, not as a son, but as a servant. So with pig stink on his clothes and a speech in his heart, the young man climbs out of the pen and takes the first step on his long journey home. But what the young man will soon discover is that his father's love is deeper and wider and greater than he could have ever fathomed.

And as a matter of fact, what we'll soon see is that this young man's speech was altogether unnecessary.

CHAPTER 7

The Return

"And he arose and came to his father."
(Luke 15:20 ESV)

The prodigal has taken off to the faraway land, his sin has left him impoverished, he's prepared a speech to beg his father's forgiveness, and now, Jesus tells us, he's finally stepped out of the pigpen and taken those first steps to return home. One of the primary reasons I wrote this book was to help prodigals like me understand the inexhaustible love of God and help them come home from any faraway land they may have traveled to. In this chapter I want to deal with some of the barriers we build up in our minds and hearts that keep us from coming home to God and living with Him, unhindered by guilt and shame after we fall into sin.

Let me begin by telling you a story of a dinner I was preparing with my friend and worship leader Aaron Ivey. Aaron and I were cooking dinner one night for all of our teaching pastors at my church; and while Aaron (one of the best chefs you'll ever meet) had me chopping onions for a corn salsa he was preparing, he said, "Matt, have you heard of this guy Jason Upton?" I hadn't so he played me a few songs from his new album, *A Table Full of Strangers, Vol. 2*. And folks, it's good. Really good.

I was just about finished with my chopping, and one of Upton's songs, "Home to Me," began to play. The theme of the song is that for believers God is our home. In other words, there is no person or place in this entire world where a child of God can experience the truest sense of home than in fellowship with God. It's a lesson I've had to learn the hard way, but it's been proven true—wonderfully and remarkably true—time after time in this prodigal's life.

When the song came to the bridge, I had stopped chopping and was just listening (maybe stop what you're doing, and go listen to it now). Upton sang these words:

> *You are where we all come from*
> *You are where we long to go*
> *We have journeyed far from Eden and we*
> *are coming home. . . .*

It's a hauntingly beautiful song, and I was crying—crying hard. Aaron asked if I was okay, and of course I blamed my tears on the onions.

Believe it or not, historically, one of the greatest struggles in my walk with Christ is believing that God might somehow give up on me because of my failures. I'm sure there is some deep psychological reason I struggle with this issue. Maybe it comes from self-doubt. Maybe it's issues I had with my parents as a child—who knows—but I've always wrestled with it. As a boy and even as a man who's been in the ministry for years, I have always had a really difficult time coming to terms with the fact that God's love for me is *unwavering*. I know all the Bible stories. I know He is faithful and just to forgive us of our sins. As a matter of fact, I know *all* the verses that tell us those thoughts are ridiculous, but I've struggled nonetheless. The more I think about it, the more it comes down to this: How could God not eventually give up on a guy who keeps failing Him? I always figured that by now—as a middle-aged guy—I'd have this Christian walk thing figured out. But I don't. And now the shortcomings that still plague me make those old familiar doubts come bubbling up.

A few years ago I was watching a panel discussion that included Dr. John Piper. On the panel someone asked him a fascinating question:

> Pastor John, is there anything in your life
> that has made you doubt God?

What a question! Here's a guy who has pastored faithfully for decades, written some of the seminal theological books of our generation, and is one of a handful of guys who are truly finishing well the race God set before him.

When he was asked that question, I honestly thought he would answer no. He's John Piper, for crying out loud. Guys like him don't doubt the goodness of God. But to my utter shock, he answered the question without a moment's hesitation.

After the question was asked, the room was dead silent as a look of sadness came over his face. He looked at the moderator and answered, "Yes, the slowness of my sanctification."

Unbelievable. Here's a man who walks with an obedience to God that most of us can only dream about, and yet the one thing that made him doubt God was the slowness in which he saw Christlikeness being perfected in him! And what started out as a shock to me melted into a deep comfort in my heart. We all have our shortcomings, doubts, failures, struggles, and hang-ups, even our heroes in the faith. And for years my hang-up has been this: How can God continue to love me when I have failed Him so many times?

One of the fascinating things I've learned about God is that He actually allows certain parts of our sanctification to occur slower than others. In other words, He *allows* His children to struggle with certain parts of their walk, sometimes even to the grave. Why? Think about it: If on the day of your salvation, God made you perfect, then you'd never again have to depend on Him! If at the moment of your salvation, He instantly took away every shortcoming, then you'd never again have to turn to God for strength—and more importantly, you'd never again have the joy of experiencing His never-ending love for His messed-up kids.

So instead of instant perfection, God allows us to have a journey of ups and downs, successes and failures, highs and lows—all with the intended design to keep us on a lifelong path of dependence and discovery of His unimaginable grace. And I've found that it's often in those seasons of the valley of the shadow of death that God teaches us lessons that stick and make the *greatest* impact on our souls. Even in our struggles, God lays out signposts along our journey, reminding us of His faithfulness. One of my many valleys was this doubt about His enduring love for me, and in this valley He spoke to me in one of the sweetest ways I've ever experienced.

I was in a season a few years ago where I was struggling again with this same old doubt; and as fate would have it, on Sunday I was supposed to preach. The text was on the never-ending love of God.

When I saw the Scripture I was supposed to preach that Sunday, I immediately began to feel a sense of crippling guilt. How can I preach about the never-ending love of God when I sometimes don't even believe it myself? Whenever I come to a situation like that—where I personally struggle with a text I'm required to preach—I usually start with an extended time of prayer. I began to cry out to God, "God, I know in my mind that You love me. And I know that through my entire life You have demonstrated that love, time and time again. But God, I don't always believe it in my heart. I've failed You too many times. Help me see and feel Your love today so I can preach to Your people with a sincere heart."

I fumbled around with my sermon for a few minutes, but nothing changed. So I walked away, hoping to start fresh the next morning.

Later that day, at lunch, a group of pastors on my team were having a discussion; and for some reason one of them brought up the question as to what were the first words we remember hearing as a child. Around the table each guy shared his earliest childhood memories. As my turn neared, I began to search my mind for the earliest memory of my childhood. Up to that point I had never given it a thought, but then it hit me.

My first memory was when I was two years old, and it was the middle of the night. I had an ear infection, and I remember being in a lot of pain. My crying woke my mother, and she picked me up from my crib, held me, and began rocking me gently in our rocking chair. It was dark in the room except for a little lamp on the table by the rocking chair. My head was lying against her arm, looking up at her face. As she rocked me, she began quietly to sing the old children's hymn.

> *When I was just a baby in my mother's*
> *arms,*
> *before I had ever run from Him,*
> *before I had ever willingly sinned or dis-*
> *obeyed God,*
> *before I had ever done anything good or*
> *righteous for His name.*

When I was just a baby, God had a message just for me.

As I sat there with my friends at the lunch table, it hit me that the first words I ever remember hearing in my entire life were "Jesus loves me." I instantly remembered my prayer from earlier that morning. "God help me see and feel Your love today so I can preach to Your people with a sincere heart." I stinking lost it. Right there at the lunch table, I started ugly crying, my chest and shoulders heaving up and down as tears fell into my barbecue. My friends asked me what in the world was wrong, and I looked up and told them the first words I ever remember hearing were that Jesus loves me. I've said a few times throughout this book that Jesus is the "love of my life." This story is why I say that. He is my first love, my greatest love, and the love that will still be mine throughout all of eternity. The story of my life is the story of His love. And as often as I forget, He is always faithful to remind me.

I can't remember much about the sermon that Sunday, but I remember telling that story. I cried again, and so did a lot of people in the congregation that day. The lyrics I heard while cooking dinner that night with Aaron Ivey were right.

God is *home* to me. And if you are His child, He is *home* to you. And no matter how many times you've forgotten or even rebelled against that truth—and no matter how many times you've let go of Him, here's a promise you can take to the bank: He will never let go of you. Friends, not believing that is the first barrier that keeps us coming home to the Lord when we fail Him. At the end of the day, when we allow our past sin to keep us from coming home to God, we do that because we think *more highly* of our sin than we do the love of God.

I have no doubt in my mind that the prodigal son was dealing with these same doubts and questions on his return from the faraway land. Have I fallen so far that my dad can't forgive me? Did my failure cross some invisible line that will put a permanent wedge between me and my father? One of the beautiful lessons the prodigal is about to discover is that it's impossible to outsin the grace of a loving Dad.

So the first barrier that often keeps us from returning to God is when we think our sin is greater than His love. But another barrier sometimes keeps God's kids from coming home, and that is we don't take our sin *seriously enough*. That was definitely not the prodigal's issue, but I've been a pastor long enough to know that for many people it is.

The Call to Mourn

Earlier in the book I talked about the Beatitudes. Jesus preached them in the Sermon on the Mount. They are a list of attitudes and attributes that define a Christian. In one of them, Jesus says, "Blessed are those who mourn, for they shall be comforted" (Matt. 5:4). The word *mourn* here is key because it's a word used specifically in regard to mourning or grieving *over our sin*. Jesus is showing us that there is a blessing and a comfort that can only be found when we mourn over our sin.

One thing critical to note is the specific word Jesus uses for our English word "mourn." It's the Greek word *pantheo*, a word that means the deepest and most heartfelt mourning a human can experience. It's a word that was most often used to describe the kind of mourning a person experiences at the loss of a loved one.

When I preached this text to my congregation, I wanted them to get a real sense as to what this kind of mourning actually looks like. I've seen with my own eyes a *pantheo*-style of mourning; and once you've seen it, you'll never forget it. The first time I remember seeing this kind of mourning was when my Aunt Sharron passed away. She was my mother's sister, but they weren't just sisters; they were identical twins. They were born in May 1944, and they were as close as I've ever seen two siblings.

True story: the first day they were ever separated in their entire lives was on my Aunt Sharron's wedding day. My Uncle Mike used to tell the story of how on their wedding night, he was anxiously awaiting the opportunity to get to do what married people do on their wedding night, but he had to wait because my aunt was crying so hard because it was the first time in her life she had been separated from my mother. That they were pretty much inseparable didn't change until a horrible day in early 1999.

I was driving to see my sister in College Station, Texas. When I walked in her door, I knew something was wrong. My sister looked at me and said, "Matt, I just got a call. Aunt Sharron and Uncle Mike were in a horrible car accident, and Aunt Sharron didn't make it."

She was my favorite aunt, and I was devastated. But things were about to get worse. At the time my mother was on her way to my sister's house to visit with us. It hit me that I was going to have to be the one to tell her of the death of her twin. When she arrived at my sister's house, I met her at the door and told her to sit down. She saw on my face that something was wrong. I said, "Mom, just sit down."

She did, and then I told her, "Mom, we just heard that Aunt Sharron was in a car accident, and she didn't make it. Mom, she died."

As soon as I said those words, a sound came out of my mother's mouth that I had never heard a human being make before and I haven't heard since. It was a low, guttural wail that involuntarily came out of her, and she collapsed into my father's arms. My father's given name is Johnny Carter, but I had never heard my mom or anyone else call him that. She always called him John. But as she collapsed into his arms, she started screaming, "Johnny, Johnny, no, no, no." That moment with my mother was the single most horrifying moment of my life, and I don't remember much after that. But that kind of grief is what I imagine when I think of *pantheo*.

Pantheo is word Jesus uses. Jesus is saying to us that when you sin, your sin shouldn't bother you. It shouldn't trouble you, but you are to grieve that sin to the level that you grieve over the death of a loved one. The response when we do? Jesus says, "Blessed are those who mourn, for they shall be comforted." Jesus teaches us that He gives a level of comfort to His children, but it can only be found on the other side of real mourning.

As you're reading this, I want you stop and think for just a second about how you respond to the sin in your life. Does your sin bother you, or does your sin cause you to mourn? I fear that far too many of us in today's culture have taken the grace of God so for granted that we've come to the place where sin is something that troubles us, but we don't *pantheo* mourn over it. We live in a Christian culture that loves to immediately jump from sin to forgiveness, but in doing so we miss the critical step of mourning.

If that's you, I want you to know that the only way I have found to see my sin in that light is when I look to the cross. When you lust after a woman in your heart. When you enter into a sexual relationship with someone not your spouse. When you respond in ungodly anger. When you allow racism to fester. When you hate. When you won't forgive. When you fall into drunkenness and debauchery. When you pursue power and privilege for personal gain. When you cheat. When you lie. When you cause dissention or conflict. Fill in the blank: when you sin, the only way I have found to truly mourn that sin is when I look to the cross.

When you look to the cross, you'll see Jesus there, the only man who has *never* sinned. You'll see Him stripped naked, tortured, and beaten within an inch of His life. When you look to the cross, you'll see nails that were driven through His hands and feet and a crown of thorns crushed into this brow. When you actually look to the cross, something will hit you. It will hit you like a thousand tons of brick that your sin put Him there. It will hit you that your Lord and Savior Jesus Christ went through all of that because of you. And only then will you mourn.

But, child of God, the amazing news is that Jesus says, "Blessed are those who mourn, for they shall be comforted." When God sees in you a real, sincere, godly mourning over your sin, He will come to you, wrap His arms around you, and bless you with a comfort that can only be found on the other side of mourning. As a matter of fact, the claim Jesus makes in the Beatitudes is that when you truly mourn your sin, you'll be happy—and not just your everyday, run of the mill kind of happy. Jesus claims you will experience the highest and best form of happiness available to us on this planet.

We're about to come to a point in the story of the prodigal son where he's at the conclusion of his long journey home, and we're going to see him finally reunited with his father. The picture Jesus paints of their reunion is simply beautiful. In my humble opinion it is the greatest picture of the love and forgiveness of our heavenly Father in all of Scripture. The reception this unimaginably sinful young man receives from his dad defies human logic and tears down any barrier we might create in our minds that we have failed too heinously or fallen too far to come back into the fold of God. God's willingness to wrap His arms of forgiveness around His sin-soiled sons and daughters comes shining through like the sun after a long storm-tossed night.

But before we go there, let me ask you a question: Have you mourned your sin? I mean, truly mourned it?

One of the things I've come to realize is that for many Christians, the reason they go on trips to the faraway land in the first place is that they've never truly come to a place where their sin grieves them. If we live in a place where we understand what our sin costs our heavenly Father and are grieved by it, then we are far less likely to walk down that road.

Maybe you are the type of person who keeps taking trips, coming home only to take another trip—then come home, then take another trip. You're without a doubt a child of God, but you have fallen into a sin pattern that keeps popping up in your life, and you can relate to Paul's words when he says, "I keep doing things I don't want to do" (see Rom. 7:19). That sin pattern might be in your life because you've never actually sat at the foot of the cross long enough to mourn. Before he came home, the prodigal son *truly* mourned his sin. And though Jesus never says as much, I have a feeling that the guy never took that same trip down the road to sin again. Sin that leads to godly sorrow produces in us a distaste for sin that is hard to forget. So, before we go any further, take some time and go to the cross. Hang out there until your sin absolutely messes you up. And when you get to that place, stand up, dry your tears, and come home. Your heavenly Father is waiting for you, and He's ready to throw you a party.

CHAPTER 8

The Reunion

Over The many years I have read and taught the story of the prodigal son, I've often wondered what the young man must have been thinking on that long walk home. Jesus describes the thoughts of the prodigal in the pigpen. We see him mourn his sin, prepare a speech where he hopes to earn a place back in this father's house as a servant, and we see him stand up and begin the journey home.

From that moment Jesus jumps immediately to the scene of his return, the incredible reunion of a sinful son and a loving father. But Jesus doesn't describe for us what must have been for the son an unimaginably nerve-racking trip. No doubt he spent a lot of time on that trip rehearsing his speech. Surely he spent a good portion of the journey beating himself up, wondering how in the world he was stupid enough to get in that horrible situation in the first place. I would guess he spent a good amount of time on his journey trying to imagine how his dad would respond, and he was probably preparing for a worst-case scenario. He no doubt wavered back and forth from feelings of uncontrollable butterflies to sickening nausea as he imagined the look on his father's face when he finally walked through the door.

While Jesus never explicitly says this was what the prodigal was thinking, I think it's safe to say from our personal experience he was anxious. And rightfully so! We all have stories from our youth of doing something wrong, messing up in some way, and having to come home and face the consequences.

I grew up in a home where my parents were pretty strict. If they told me to do something, they expected me to follow their instructions to the letter, and any deviation from their wishes usually resulted in some pretty severe consequences.

I remember one night in my final year of high school. My buddies were hanging out at a friend's house and invited me over. I asked my mom's permission and she agreed. Before I left, she told me to be home by midnight. I don't remember exactly what we were doing that night, but I lost track of time, and at about 11:40 I realized I better head home. Well, it turns out that it takes exactly twenty-two minutes to get from my friend's front door to mine. I walked in the door at 12:02, and Shirley Ann Carter was standing in the doorway with her arms folded. When I saw her face, I knew I was in trouble. "What time did I tell you to come home?" she asked. I responded, "Twelve o-clock." She turned and pointed to the time on the microwave that now said 12:03. "What time is it right now?" she said with her voice growing in frustration. "12:03," I responded, realizing this might not end well.

She began to inform me that I was grounded for the weekend because I disobeyed her. I instantly began to protest. I tried to argue that there was no way to tell if the microwave clock was even accurate (this was before we all had cell phones set to a universal time). She informed me that the time on the microwave was considered the letter of the law. So that didn't work. I also tried to explain that I, in no way, was being rebellious, and I thought I left in plenty of time to get home. That didn't work either.

Looking back at that night, who knows what caused my mother to respond so harshly? Maybe she had a bad day and was taking it out on me. Maybe she was in an argument with my dad and was just in a bad mood. Maybe in those two or three minutes before I walked in the door she was imagining the worst-case scenario where I had been in an accident. Who knows? The point I'm trying to make is that we all have stories of authority figures in our lives responding in anger, even when we didn't deserve it.

So you can imagine what was going through the prodigal's mind on his return home. Whatever punishment or response was coming his way, he *did* deserve, and he knew it. He wasn't returning home a couple of minutes late after an evening with his buddies; he was returning home after a long trip of outright rebellion. No doubt the guy was nervous and rightly so.

This wayward young man soon discovered that every second of that long journey home he spent in fear and self-loathing was completely unfounded. For waiting for him was not a father who had written him off, or a father who had his arms folded in disgust. Rather, waiting for him at home was a father who loved him with a love so fierce and a grace so unending that they were beyond his ability to comprehend.

I think the best way to walk through this beautiful part of the story is to go step-by-step, looking carefully at the words of Jesus as He describes the prodigal's return.

The young man has finally completed his journey.

> He's rounding the last bend to the house,
> and he can see it now.
>
> Still in the distance.
>
> The house, the front porch.
>
> The livestock gently grazing in the green grass of the pastures that lead to his abandoned home.

The familiarity of the scene no doubt gave him a sense of relief mixed with the wild uncertainty of what might unfold in the next few minutes.

He looks again at his home growing closer by the second, and then he sees something he could have never expected. Still in the distance, standing there on the front porch, is his father. The son is still a long way away, but yes, it's unmistakable now. It's his dad, standing there, hand shielding his eyes from the sun, looking intently in the distance. The young man's heart undoubtedly began to pound in his chest. The moment he had dreaded was finally here, and what happened next would change his life forever.

Luke 15:20 says, "But while he was still a long way off, his father saw him and felt compassion" (ESV).

When I have taught this story from the pulpit, I have often ignored this simple yet profound phrase, moving quickly to their reunion. But this phrase is so critical in our understanding about how God deals with us in our sin.

Jesus tells us that "while he was still a long way off, the father saw him." Let me pause here and make something clear about the story of the prodigal son. The father in this story represents God. And the prodigal son represents us, His sons and daughters who have bought the lie that there is a better life for us outside of His love. And this simple phrase, "But while he was still a long way off, his father saw him and felt compassion," teaches us something invaluable about how God deals with us in the midst of our rebellion.

Those words teach us that this father (who represents God) had been betrayed in a way that is beyond comprehension. Yet, despite all the ways his son had wounded him, he never stopped looking, never stopped straining His eyes toward the distance, hoping against hope that one day he would look up and see his son walking over the horizon. In this story Jesus is teaching us that we have a heavenly Dad who *never* gives up on His kids. This one phrase shows us that the father spent his days and nights going about his everyday routine but all the while pausing, stopping, and looking down the road with the hope that his son would one day come home. Unlike too many people in our lives, our God never reaches a point where He gives up and stops hoping, looking, and waiting for our return.

Never.

Why, you might ask, does a perfectly holy God, who actually has the right to be upset, not deal with us harshly?

Because He is not our earthly parents, or our spouses, or our friends. No matter how loving, human love has limits, and we often project our views of human love on God. Have you ever been tempted to think that you've messed up so badly or so frequently that God will throw up His hands and say, "Enough!"? I have. And in one sense it's a rational fear. We live in a world where other people's love for us most certainly has its limits. As humans we have breaking points. We have imaginary lines drawn in the sand that if someone we're in a relationship with crosses, our love can diminish or even disappear. Some of you might have even experienced that horrible reality with a parent, a friend, or even a spouse; and so it's hard not to project that fear onto God when we have crossed some pretty serious lines. But Jesus is teaching us in this story that is simply not how God works. When it comes to His kids, God has no lines we can cross where He says, "Enough!" It's never going to happen. Are there consequences for our sin? Absolutely. But one of them will never be a heavenly Father who says, "I'm done loving you."

The apostle Paul spoke of this unending love of God. He said, "For I am convinced that neither death, nor life, nor angels, nor principalities, nor things present, nor things to come, nor powers, nor height, nor depth, nor any other created thing, will be able to separate us from the love of God, which in in Christ Jesus our Lord" (Rom. 8:38–39).

Is God holy? Yes, but we must never forget that He is also a God of love, a love the Scriptures say is limitless, *never-ending* toward His children.

Another way to think about it is this: God's love for you is stronger than your sin. Can you just stop and read that again? His love for you is stronger than your sin. When your sin comes, and it comes strong and hard—His love is stronger. When your love for Him wavers, His love for you stands firm. When your love for Him waxes and wanes, His love for you keeps coming in as strong and faithful as the ocean tides. And what Jesus just told us is that when you turn your eyes away from Him, He turns His eyes toward you, waiting patiently for your return.

Brothers and sisters in Christ, can you hear that today—and not just hear it but believe it? What the Holy Spirit-inspired Word of God just told you is that God *can't* stop loving you deeply and profoundly. It's literally impossible. He can no more stop loving you than He can stop being God. So while we are on our ridiculous trips to the faraway land, He doesn't turn around and walk away in disgust. It's exactly quite the opposite. Jesus is showing us in this story that at the moment of our rebellion He turns His eyes to the horizon and won't stop watching and waiting for you until He sees your face.

The God Who Won't Turn Away

I want to take a minute to share with you why, in the midst of our rebellion, God actually turns His face not away from you but toward you. Why, unlike too many people in our life, who when we hurt them, turn their back and give up, He does the opposite. The answer is found at the cross of Christ. Years ago I preached a series at my church about the seven sayings of Jesus on the cross. Jesus hung on the cross for six hours, and during those six hours He only said seven things. Each one of them has meaning and purpose, and there is much to be learned through them. Toward the end of those six hours, He hung there in agony, and the time for His death was approaching. The sky began to grow dark, and all of a sudden Jesus cried out, "My God, My God, why have You forsaken Me?" (Matt. 27:46).

Throughout the centuries since that moment, there have been countless debates as to the meaning of this statement by Jesus. One thing is for certain: He was fulfilling a prophecy from the book of Psalms where the Messiah was beaten and forsaken. But there is a theory about the moment that has become one of the most accepted explanations for why Jesus cried out that God was forsaking Him. To fully understand this theory, let me give you some background context.

One of the things we know about Jesus is that He has existed eternally with God in a perfect relationship of love, completely unhindered by sin. You see, when you think about what creates tension in relationships, it's always sin. But the Father and the Son have, for all eternity, never experienced that strife. For all eternity, they have been together in a perfect, sinless relationship. And

Scripture teaches us that while Jesus was on the cross, *He became our sin.* A lot of songs out there talk about how Jesus "took our sin upon His shoulders," but that is not entirely accurate. The Bible says He *became* our sin. Every single sin that has ever been committed, He took it to the cross. Every rape, every murder, every theft, every moment of lust and pride and hate. He bore that sin to the fullest on the cross.

As I shared earlier in the book, sin separates. So as Jesus became our sin on the cross, that was the first moment in *all of eternity* that the Father and son were separated. Theologians throughout the centuries have speculated that while Jesus hung on the cross, becoming our sin, God turned His face away. He couldn't bear to see it. That's why Jesus cried out, "My God, My God, why have You forsaken Me?"

So here's the point I'm trying to make: Jesus was forsaken by God so that you won't ever have to be. God turned His face away from Jesus on the cross so that God would never, ever have to turn His face away from you. My friends, if you have trusted in Christ as your Lord and Savior, Jesus paid for every single one of your sins on the cross. So now, because of Jesus, when we stupidly run to sin, God doesn't turn away from us. *He turns toward us.* The cross of Jesus ensures you that no matter how far you've fallen, no matter how far you've run, God is looking right at you with love, hoping you will return to Him.

And how does God respond to us when He finally sees us coming home from the faraway land? Watch what happens next.

The God Who Runs

> "And he arose and came to his father. But while he was still a long way off, his father saw him and felt compassion, and ran and embraced him and kissed him." (Luke 15:20 ESV)

With these words Jesus shows us that all our fears about a God waiting to punish or shame or rebuke us because of our sin are simply wrong on their face. When the father looked at the horizon, maybe for the thousandth time, and finally saw his son walking home, he responds in a way that ought to bring tears into the eyes of sinners like you and me.

When the father sees his son finally returning, his first response was not to think to himself, *Well, there he is. The loser has finally come to his senses.* The father doesn't turn around and shout to the people in the house, "Hey, ya'll remember my son? Yeah, the one who took all my money and blew it. He's back. Let's see how this turns out."

No. Those responses are how sinful people respond to sinful people.

Jesus tells us that when the father finally saw the son, he hiked up his robes around his waist and took off on a dead sprint toward his son. Can you stop and imagine that for a second? The dad was probably pretty old at that point.

As I write this book, I'm forty-five years old, and I already have arthritis in both my knees. I avoid running at all cost because when I do, my knees swell up, and I pay the price for days. No doubt the old man was just like me. It has probably been years since he jogged, much less *ran*. But that's exactly what happened when the father saw the son. It was an uncontrollable response. He threw age, dignity, and caution to the wind and took off in a dead sprint toward his son.

As a guy who was in ROTC in college, I've always been a sucker for those videos you see on YouTube of a man or woman who serves in the armed forces returning home from a long deployment to their family. When the soldier steps off the plane and walks into the terminal of the airport, and their eyes meet their families for the first time in ages, what happens? The family flings their arms in the air and takes off running toward their loved one. When they finally reach each other, their embrace is so fierce that they almost knock each other over. Tears start flowing as they embrace, holding onto each other like they will never let go.

You see, in those first moments of their reunion, nothing else in the world matters but the one fact that their loved one has finally returned. Here's a question for you: Are those soldiers and their families' relationships perfect? No. They have arguments and problems and history just like everybody else. But in that one moment, only one thing matters. They are finally together, and that love they have for one another absolutely overwhelms everything else. And in this story that is how God responds to His rebellious son. He sees him and runs to him and almost knocks him over with an embrace of love.

Friends, this story teaches us something profound about how God thinks about us. Our separation from Him hurts Him more than our sin. Does our sin hurt the heart of God? Yes. Of course it does. But what Jesus is trying to teach us through this picture of a running God is that there is something He longs for more than anything else. He wants you near to Him. He wants you home where you belong. And when you finally return, joy fills His heart that overwhelms anything you might have done in your past.

The God of Mercy and Grace

The story could have easily ended there, and with that ending we could all put to rest any doubt in our hearts about how God responds to us in our sin. But Jesus doesn't end the story there. As the father embraced the son, the son began to give his "please forgive me, make me one of your hired hands" speech that he had prepared in the pigpen. The son pulled the father away and said, "Father, I have sinned against heaven and before you. I am no longer worthy to be called your son" (Luke 15:21 ESV). But Jesus tells us the father *ignores* the speech. He doesn't even respond to it. Rather the father turned around and shouted to his servants, "Bring quickly the best robe, and put it on him, and put a ring on his hand, and shoes on his feet. And bring the fatted calf and kill it, and let us eat and celebrate" (Luke 15:22–23 ESV). The father completely ignores the son's request to make him a hired hand and instead instantly lavishes the son with gifts of a robe, a ring, new shoes, and a party.

This moment in this story gives us one of the most beautiful descriptions of the grace of God in all the Bible. Why? Because who gives hugs and robes and rings to rebellious sons and daughters returning from a long trip of outright rebellion? Our God does. The Bible has a word for how God deals with us like that: it's called grace.

So let's take a minute and talk about the grace of God. It's what He gives us when we return home to Him from our sin. I've noticed that although *grace* is a word that we have heard countless times, it's a concept that is difficult to understand and even more difficult to believe.

Grace is an interesting word because we hear it in sermons and in songs and see it over and over in Scripture, but unfortunately it's a concept that most of us don't fully have our minds around.

Years ago I heard a sermon by Pastor Tony Evans where he explained the difference between mercy and grace. I've never forgotten it because it helped me grasp the concept of grace like never before. Pastor Evans, who is a master at sermon analogy, asked his listeners to imagine that we had been pulled over by a policeman for speeding. When he pulled us over, he tells us that we were going twenty miles per hour over the limit. He asked the question, "What if, when the police officer pulled you over and explained that you were going twenty miles per hour over the limit, he looked at you and said, 'You know what, I'm feeling generous today, so I'm not going to give you a ticket.'" Pastor Evans asked, "Is that mercy or grace?"

He explained that would actually be mercy. Mercy is when we *do not receive something we deserve.*

But then he said, "What if, when the police officer said, 'I'm not going to give you a ticket, but I tell you what, it's cold outside, so I'm going to go back to my car and get my coat and give it to you.'"

And then when the police officer returned with his coat, he pulled out his wallet and said, "I see that your gas tank is almost on empty. Here's twenty bucks. Go fill up your car."

Pastor Evans then explained that is not mercy but grace. He taught us that while mercy is when you *don't* receive something you *do deserve*, grace is when you *do* receive something *you don't deserve.*

Listen to the words of the Gospel writer John. He wrote, "For from his [God's] fullness we have all received, grace upon grace" (John 1:16 ESV).

And friends, if you take anything away from reading this book, I want you to take away this: When we sin and rebel against God, He shows us mercy. Scripture says that "the wages of sin is death" (Rom. 6:23). In other words, when we sin, we earn death. But the verse continues and says, "But the free gift of God is eternal life in Jesus Christ our Lord." That's mercy. We all have sinned and deserve death, but He doesn't give us what we deserve. But the amazing thing about God is He doesn't stop there. He doesn't just not give us what we do deserve, but He goes further—He *gives us instead what we don't deserve.*

Grace upon grace.

I love how the apostle Paul describes this grace God gives us.

He writes, "But God, being rich in mercy, because of the great love with which he loved us, even when we were dead in our trespasses, made us alive together with Christ—by grace you have been saved—and raised us up with him and seated us with him in the heavenly places in Christ Jesus, so that in the coming ages he might show the immeasurable *riches of his grace* in kindness toward us in Christ Jesus" (Eph 2:4–7 ESV; emphasis added).

Our God doesn't retaliate against us or shame us in our sin but rather shows us mercy in Christ. And if that were not enough, He keeps going. He lavishes us with grace upon grace that we simply don't deserve.

When we finally understand the grace of God—that God not only doesn't give us what we do deserve but lavishes upon us gifts we don't deserve—then we start to see that John Newton, the old hymn writer, got it right when he wrote: "Amazing grace, how sweet the sound, that saved a wretch like me. I once was lost but now am found, was blind, but now I see." He's right. Grace truly is amazing. And if you've grown up in church, you've probably sung that song a hundred times. But I bet you didn't know that last line, "I once was lost but now am found," came from the story of the prodigal son. Let's look at the last thing the father says before he throws the son a party.

The Amazing Grace of God

The son has come home. The father ran to him, embraced him, and clothed him with a robe and a ring. He ordered his servants to kill a fatted calf and prepare for the party of the year. But before the party begins, the father says one more thing:

> "For this my son was dead, and is alive again; he was lost, and is found." (Luke 15:24 ESV)

With those final words of the father, Jesus is teaching us one final lesson. A benediction of sorts sums up and ties a bow on everything He hoped we learned from the story of the prodigal son. In a way this is Jesus' thesis sentence—one sentence that encapsulates the grand lesson of the entire parable. The father says, "My son was dead, and is alive again." With those words Jesus is making a bold and final claim. The faraway land of sin equals death. At home with the Father equals life.

Jesus told this whole story to get to that one final sentence; and my friends, it's a sentence you must decide whether you believe. Jesus is making the claim that there is no life in sin. It only leads to death. But on the other hand—life, the fullness of life—can be found in one place and one place alone: at home with your heavenly Father. Jesus believed it, I believe it, and the prodigal son now believes it. The question is, do you?

In the first chapter of this book, I said that the younger generation is having to ask questions sooner and more often than maybe any generation before them. Questions like, If I go all-in with Christ, is it really going to be worth it? If I stay at home with my heavenly Father, am I experiencing the best life has to offer? The father's final statement answers these questions once and for all. Life is found in one place and one place alone. At home with your heavenly Father.

My prayer is that this book will serve as all the evidence you need. I pray that regardless of where you are in your journey these words will be enough to anchor your heart to God and never let go. You'll never regret it if you do.

I remember the exact moment in my life when I finally surrendered to believing that trying to find life in any place but Him was a monumental waste of time. It was just a normal Sunday at my church, and a friend of mine was preaching. He was preaching about Jacob, a man who constantly ran from God, trying to find his own better way. Toward the end of the sermon my friend said something I've never forgotten.

Throughout the sermon he'd been preaching with power and conviction, but when he got to this line, his voice grew soft and his cadence slow. He all but whispered, "Jacob finally discovered something about the nature of God. Jacob let go of God, but God never let go of Jacob."

When he said those words, something broke inside me in the best possible way. I spent the remainder of the church service thinking about all the times in my life when I let go of God. It was a pretty long list. I thought of all the times throughout my life that I bought the lie that there was a better life for me outside of the love of the Father and I had to take a trip to the faraway land to discover that simply wasn't true. And then I thought about all the times I came limping home, smelling like a pigpen, only to find the Lord scanning the horizon, waiting to run to me when He saw me round that final turn home. And in that moment on the front row of my church, I said to myself quietly, almost as a prayer, "God, I believe this. I've let go of You a thousand times, but You've never let go of me."

I've not been perfect since that moment. But I can tell you that I'm different now. I no longer believe the lies Satan whispers in my ear. I'm utterly convinced that the best life I can ever find is at home with my heavenly Father. If I've learned anything, I've learned this: God *is* my home.

So if, as you read this, you are scanning the horizon, looking at the faraway land, wondering if a better life is waiting for you there, don't go. Take it from a man who's been there before. God is better. It's really not even close.

And if you're reading this and you know beyond a shadow of a doubt that you are His son or daughter but you find yourself today in the faraway land of sin, come home right now. Don't wait a single second longer. God is waiting and watching for you. From the moment you left, He never stopped. So stand up, walk out of the pigpen, skip the speech writing—He's going to ignore it anyway—and come home.

When He sees you, He'll run to you, wrap His arms around you, and remind you of His never-ending love. And as you stand there, finally home, being lavished with the mercy and grace of the God of the universe, you'll discover something that will forever change your life. There's no better place in all the world than in the arms of your Father.

Acknowledgments

I'd like to thank Devin Maddox and Lindsey Lundin for your work on editing this project. Your thoughts and additions helped make this a much better book.

I'd also like to thank the elders and pastors of The Austin Stone who do the daily, sometimes thankless work of shepherding God's flock in Austin and around the world. There is no other group of men on this planet I'd rather be in the fight with than you.

My wife Jennifer has modeled the grace of God to me on countless occasions and been a constant source of encouragement, love, and support. And finally, I'd like to thank my Lord and Savior Jesus Christ. When I was lost, You left the ninety-nine and found me.

Jesus has been the love of my life, my dearest and oldest Friend, without whom I'd have no story to tell.

About The Author

Matt Carter serves as the pastor of preaching and vision at The Austin Stone Community Church in Austin, Texas, which has grown from a core team of fifteen to more than eight thousand attending each Sunday since he planted it in 2002. Matt has coauthored multiple books including a commentary on the Gospel of John in The Christ Centered Exposition Commentary series. Matt also coauthored a novel of historical fiction, *Steal Away Home*, which tells the real-life story of famed pastor Charles Spurgeon's unlikely friendship with former slave-turned-missionary Thomas Johnson. Matt holds the MDiv from Southwestern Seminary and a doctorate in expositional preaching from Southeastern Seminary. He and his wife Jennifer have been married for more than twenty years, and they have three children—John Daniel, Annie, and Samuel.